I0808272

GREAT AMERICAN THINKERS

Harriet Beecher Stowe

Author and Abolitionist

Katie Griffiths

Cavendish Square
New York

Published in 2017 by Cavendish Square Publishing, LLC
243 5th Avenue, Suite 136, New York, NY 10016

Copyright © 2017 by Cavendish Square Publishing, LLC

First Edition

No part of this publication may be reproduced, stored in a retrieval system, or transmitted in any form or by any means—electronic, mechanical, photocopying, recording, or otherwise—without the prior permission of the copyright owner. Request for permission should be addressed to Permissions, Cavendish Square Publishing, 243 5th Avenue, Suite 136, New York, NY 10016. Tel (877) 980-4450; fax (877) 980-4454.

Website: cavendishsq.com

This publication represents the opinions and views of the author based on his or her personal experience, knowledge, and research. The information in this book serves as a general guide only. The author and publisher have used their best efforts in preparing this book and disclaim liability rising directly or indirectly from the use and application of this book.

CPSIA Compliance Information: Batch #CS16CSQ

All websites were available and accurate when this book was sent to press.

Cataloging-in-Publication Data

Names: Griffiths, Katie.
Title: Harriet Beecher Stowe: author and abolitionist / Katie Griffiths.
Description: New York : Cavendish Square, 2017. | Series: Great American thinkers | Includes index.
Identifiers: ISBN 9781502619303 (library bound) | ISBN 9781502619310 (ebook)
Subjects: LCSH: Stowe, Harriet Beecher, 1811-1896--Juvenile literature. | Authors, American--19th century--Biography--Juvenile literature. | Abolitionists--United States--Biography--Juvenile literature. | United States--History--Civil War, 1861-1865--Literature and the war--Juvenile literature.
Classification: LCC PS2956.G75 2017 | DDC 813'.3--dc23

Editorial Director: David McNamara
Editor: Elizabeth Schmermund
Copy Editor: Rebecca Rohan
Art Director: Jeffrey Talbot
Designer: Amy Greenan
Production Assistant: Karol Szymczuk
Photo Research: J8 Media

The photographs in this book are used by permission and through the courtesy of: Google Cultural Institute/File:Alanson Fisher - Harriet Beecher Stowe - Google Art Project.jpg/Wikimedia Commons, cover; James F. Gibson/File:Yorktown artillery2.jpg/Wikimedia Commons, 4; Gurney & Sons/File:Harriet Beecher Stowe c1852.jpg/Wikimedia Commons, 6; Universal History Archive/Getty Images, 8; Hulton Archive/Getty Images, 11; © North Wind Picture Archives, 14; John L. Magee/File:Forcing Slavery Freesoilers Throats.jpg/Wikimedia Commons, 16; Yale University Art Gallery/File:Eli Whitney by Samuel Finley Breese Morse 1822.jpg/Wikimedia Commons, 17; Hulton Archive/Getty Images, 20; Library of Congress pga.00675/File:Cotton plantation on the Mississippi, 1884 (cropped).jpg/Wikimedia Commons, 25; Richard Cavalleri/Shutterstock.com, 28; Schlesinger Library, Radcliffe Institute, Harvard University/Bridgeman Images, 32; AlexPlank/File:Beecherc.jpg/Wikimedia Commons, 34; Unknown/File:Hartford female seminary.jpg/Wikimedia Commons, 35; © Mary Evans Picture Library/Alamy Stock Photo, 40; Library of Congress cwpbh.02529/File:Lyman Beecher - Brady-Handy.jpg/Wikimedia Commons, 45; Midnightdreary/File:Stowe, Harriet Beecher grave.jpg/Wikimedia Commons, 46; David and Lydia Child/File:National Anti-Slavery Standard Newspaper January 7, 1841.jpg/Wikimedia Commons, 48; Schlesinger Library, Radcliffe Institute, Harvard University/Bridgeman Images, 52; Unknown/File:Theodore Dwight Weld.jpg/Wikimedia Commons, 53; Everett Historical/Shutterstock.com, 55; Picture courtesy of The Harriet Beecher Stowe Center, Hartford, Connecticut/File:Edward Beecher.jpg/Wikimedia Commons, 56; Charles Willson Peale/File:Charles Willson Peale, American - Portrait of John and Elizabeth Lloyd Cadwalader and their Daughter Anne - Google Art Project.jpg/Wikimedia Commons, 60; Everett Historical/Shutterstock.com, 62; Universal History Archive/Getty Images, 65; Universal History Archive/Getty Images, 68; © ClassicStock/Alamy Stock Photo, 78; Samuel J. Miller/File:Frederick Douglass by Samuel J Miller, 1847-52.png/Wikimedia Commons, 82; Bentley Historical Library/File:Henry Bibb.png/Wikimedia Commons, 86; Mary Henderson Eastman/File:Aunt Phillis's Cabin.jpg/Wikimedia Commons, 90; loc#113990/Library of congress, 95; © AF archive/Alamy Stock Photo, 96; Chordboard/File:CC No 15 Uncle Toms Cabin.jpg/Wikimedia Commons, 99; Project Gutenberg/File:Huck and jim on raft.jpg/Wikimedia Commons, 100; Allan warren/File:James Baldwin 37 Allan Warren.jpg/Wikimedia Commons, 103; Olga Besnard/Shutterstock.com, 105.

Printed in the United States of America

CONTENTS

INTRODUCTION

A Momentous Event

In 1863, President Lincoln finally signed the **Emancipation** Proclamation. This single action freed more than three million enslaved people in slaveholding Southern states. As the news spread across the country and reached Boston, a single voice inside the packed Music Hall began to chant "Harriet Beecher Stowe! Harriet Beecher Stowe!" Soon, the rest of crowd picked up the refrain as they turned to face a small, middle-aged woman standing up on the balcony. It was Harriet Beecher Stowe. The people in the crowd, like many who knew of her work, felt instinctively that this woman had helped to bring about such a momentous event.

Best known for her novel *Uncle Tom's Cabin*, Stowe is an important figure within the history of race relations in America, and also in the wider history of the country. She hailed from

Many historians believe Stowe's novel, *Uncle Tom's Cabin*, to have been a key trigger of the American Civil War.

Harriet Beecher Stowe was to follow in her family's tradition of political activism.

a family of reformers and activists who understood the power of language and argument. The Beechers were one of the most influential families of the nineteenth century, and Harriet did not shrink from the opportunity to make a name for herself. She was intensely interested both in the issues of her time and in how she could personally make an impact. She felt a great personal responsibility to help resolve the problems she saw in the world and believed to do so was simply part of her civic duty.

Uncle Tom's Cabin was just one of her attempts to affect change in her contemporary society. Most historians now perceive the novel as one of the greatest feats of persuasion in American history. By tackling the barriers her peers had built up against abolishing slavery, she worked to turn the general public to the cause of abolition. Her words forced her readers to examine their own prejudices and lack of action and elevated black characters to a position of moral and ethical superiority that no white writer before had previously attempted. She inspired nationwide debate and dialogue, bringing the issue into greater prominence by the book's runaway success. Both supporters and critics would later point to her novel as one of the key triggers of the Civil War.

Yet, it is interesting that today Harriet Beecher Stowe has become mostly lost from the national memory, that the names of her noble heroes have become racial slurs, and that a woman once championed by none other than the noted black abolitionist Frederick Douglass is now perceived by some as a racist. Her novel, once a beacon of progressive thought, is now seen as the source of some of the most offensive black stereotypes.

The story of Harriet Beecher Stowe and her work is complex and worthy of greater study. While her views and characters may not have weathered the storm of time, they are an important and necessary piece of American race history. They give us invaluable insight into the conditions and perceptions of slavery in **antebellum** America, as well as providing the starting point for debates that are still relevant today—such as the portrayal of African Americans in the media. Even in the twenty-first century, Stowe's critics and supporters must realize that a debate that does not acknowledge her contributions can never give a full picture of America's past and present.

CHAPTER ONE

Stowe's America

Harriet Beecher Stowe was born into one of the most defining periods of American history. America was not only cementing its national identity, but developing its political relationships with the rest of the world. The late eighteenth and early nineteenth centuries saw a brutal clash of political and social forces—a mixture of high-level governmental battles and **grassroots activism**. It was on this battlefield that Stowe would come to play a significant role. But how was she prepared for her task? Was she **innately** revolutionary or did the time and place she resided in shape her ideas?

The historical and social conditions of her time clearly had a great impact on her. Three hugely significant factors were the establishment and evolution of slavery in the United States, the rise of the abolition movement, and the growing tensions

Slaves were most commonly used as plantation labor in Southern states.

between the Northern and Southern states in the buildup to the Civil War. Combined, these conditions led Stowe down a path of political activism and literary success that would in turn continue to impact her own country, even long after her death. However, in order to understand Harriet Beecher Stowe and her work in context, it is important to examine how these factors of slavery, the abolition movement, and the North-South political divide were born and evolved over time.

Slavery in the United States

The story of the American slave trade began in the early seventeenth century. In 1619, the town of Jamestown in Virginia was the site of the first documented slaves entering what was then the British North American colonies. Roughly twenty captive Africans were brought ashore from the ship and sold into slavery. However, the official beginning of colonial North America's slave trade occurred some years later when, in 1629, the *Desire*, the first American slave carrier, was built and launched in Massachusetts. Over the next three centuries, around twelve million Africans were kidnapped from their native countries and forced onto slave ships. Only 10.5 million survived the arduous trip to their destination.

This century would prove to be both a formative period for American slavery and also its most defining. In her book *The Abolitionist Movement*, author Claudine Ferrell argues that it was this century that ultimately shaped the legal course of slavery in America:

> Rights held by colonials in general were steadily denied slaves in the formal slave codes that appeared near the turn of the eighteenth century. Applying to free and slave blacks alike, the codes legitimized and organized a racial labor system that had generally developed without the benefit of laws. The system made slaves chattel (property) of a master who held total dominance.

as slave ports. In 1750, Georgia was the last of the British North American colonies to legalize slavery.

The Long Climb

By the end of the 1700s, racial oppression had been codified into the country's laws by restricting the movement, marriage, and work of African Americans, and violent rebellions and uprisings had increased dramatically. However, change was in the air. The year 1767 saw the Virginia House of Burgess boycott the British slave trade, and Georgia and the Carolinas soon followed. In 1772, the very first autobiographical slave narrative was published in Britain. The book, titled *A narrative of the most remarkable particulars in the life of James Albert Ukawsaw Gronniosaw, an African prince, as related by himself*, was written by a man who had been captured from his native land of Bornu (modern-day Nigeria) before being sold into slavery. He was transported to Barbados and eventually bought by an evangelical preacher. Though often criticized for its lack of antislavery **rhetoric**, it was still the first time that a black slave had given voice to his own experiences, and Gronniosaw became the first published black author in Britain. Between 1774 and 1775, Connecticut, Rhode Island, Georgia, and Virginia all took action against the importation of slaves. In 1777, Vermont became the first of the thirteen colonies to abolish slavery and enfranchise all adult males.

Then, in 1787, the Northwest Territory made slavery illegal through the passage of a bill called the Northwest Ordinance. This territory was one of the first organized sections of the United States and covered an area that would later become the six states of Ohio, Indiana, Illinois, Michigan, Wisconsin, and Minnesota. This may have seemed to some at the time like a tipping point. However, it was merely the first step in a new battle. The Northwest Ordinance outlawed slavery except as criminal punishment and was only applicable in the Northwest Territory. Furthermore, residents of the territory were still required to return fugitive slaves to slaveholding territories. In the same year, the US Constitution was drafted with provisions for slave states. It included a section stating that the slave trade would not be banned until 1808. A few years later, in order to protect the newly formed and still fragile union of states, a new federal law was passed enforcing the return of slaves who had escaped and crossed state lines. Nationwide abolition still had a very long way to go.

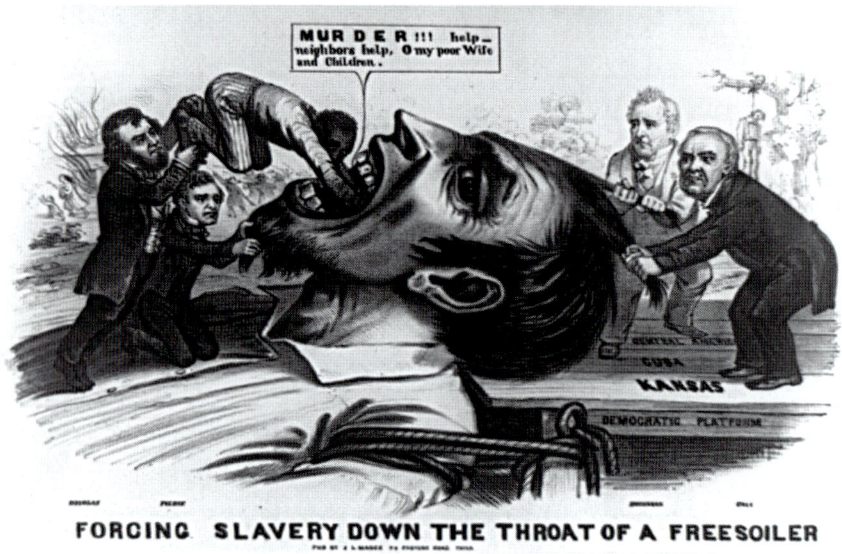

The issue of slavery was widely discussed in the contemporary media and became a political issue in national debates.

As the North began to turn away from slave labor, demand in the South continued to increase. In 1793, Eli Whitney invented the cotton gin—a machine that could quickly and easily separate cotton fibers from their seeds. This seemingly simple object revolutionized the cotton industry in the United States, vastly decreasing processing time and increasing production rates. However, the upturn in productivity led to a massive growth in slavery as demand for cotton workers reached an all-time high. Between the years of 1790 and 1850, the number of slaves rose from 700,000 to 3.2 million. Some

Eli Whitney's invention of the cotton gin spurred rates of slave labor to new heights.

historians have even claimed that the stress placed on the slave trade by this phenomenal increase in demand contributed to the outbreak of the American Civil War.

Unfinished Business

The importation of slaves was banned by the US Congress in 1808, but this did little to address the day-to-day system of slavery that was still alive and well in many parts of America. When looking back at this period with modern eyes, it is hard to be anything but horrified at the practice, to be left cold by the behavior of white slaveholders, and to be confused and outraged by a placidly accepting white public. However, during the seventeenth and eighteenth century, there was very little moral self-doubt or hesitation from slaveholders or the general public. Some actually thought the system to be necessary and beneficial to African Americans. Many more believed themselves to be God-fearing citizens operating within the guidelines of Christianity, with little fear that future generations might shrink in horror at their callous actions. Yet, within the next century, the system of slavery would end in a blaze of outrage, political activism, and public disgust. How was this accomplished? What voices raised the battle cry? How did that call to arms grow?

The American Abolitionist Movement

In his book *American Abolitionists*, Stanley Harold defines abolitionists as simply:

> [P]eople—black and white, female and male—who during the eighteenth and nineteenth centuries sought to end slavery and secure racial justice. They were part of a broader struggle within the Atlantic World against the enslavement of Africans and people of African descent.

Harold's focus on American abolitionists as part of a wider force is important. Abolitionism was a movement with many faces and voices, and it spread out across several countries. His emphasis on the importance and necessity of group action and collaboration cannot be stressed enough. Even within the United States, the movement consisted of many different groups—free blacks, the Quakers, revolutionaries, and, later, many people in the free Northern states. Each group had its own ideas about how to best affect change, and their political tactics often evolved over the centuries, responding to events as they unfolded. Though the schools of thought within abolitionism were numerous, there are two key periods that characterized the ideology, tactics, and strategy of these activists: gradualism and immediatism.

Gradualism

Since its origin in the seventeenth century, Africans and African Americans have sought to escape from slavery. Famous examples include the 1712 New York Slave Revolt, the 1739 Stono Rebellion in South Carolina, and the 1791 Mina Conspiracy in Louisiana. The first signs of real protest from the white population of America appeared at the end of the seventeenth century, although change did not occur for many years.

In 1671, English dissenter George Fox, founder of the Religious Society of Friends, began to sow agitation amongst his fellow Quakers by speaking out against slaveholding to other society members while on a visit to North America. The Quakers would become a key protest group in the early abolition movement. Over the next hundred years, Quaker antislavery societies would champion legal measures designed to encourage the gradual abolition of slavery. This led to the movement's name of "gradualism." The first Quaker antislavery society, and indeed the world's first, was established in 1775. It was known as the Pennsylvania Society for Promoting the Abolition of Slavery (PAS), and Benjamin Franklin would later become its honorary president in 1787. Other famous members include the English-American political activist Thomas Paine and Founding Father Benjamin Rush.

George Fox, seen here preaching in a tavern, encouraged his fellow Quakers to adopt antislavery views and lifestyles.

ABOLITION, GRADUALISM, AND COLONIZATION

Abolition is a term that is often confusing to those attempting to understand the politics of the American antislavery movement during the 1800s. The average dictionary defines it as an umbrella term meaning "the legal prohibition and ending of slavery." However this term began as only one part of a larger movement, and it is important to understand both its meaning and the other ideologies with which it worked.

One important movement within abolition was colonization. This was a belief in the relocation of black people back to African countries. The American Colonization Society, otherwise known as the "American Society for Colonizing the Free People of Color of the United States," was an organization that worked to transport freeborn blacks and emancipated slaves to Africa. It was founded in 1816 by a group of influential men, including Frances Scott Key, Henry Clay, and the Presbyterian minister Robert Finley. Local and state governments largely supported this organization, as well as churches, and even the federal government contributed some initial funding. Unsurprisingly, its membership was mainly white and even included a large number of slaveholders. The prevailing view of the society was that free blacks could not integrate with white American society. The Society's activities focused on the buying and freeing of slaves, as well as paying for their passage to the west coast of Africa. In 1821, the organization was granted land in the Cape Mesurado area in order to establish a colony for the transported freed slaves. This would later become Monrovia, Liberia.

Supporters of colonization perceived the movement as both **humanitarian** and also a practical means of ending slavery. However, many abolitionists and African Americans fiercely opposed this practice. They believed that it would only result in the loss of the best of the free black population, while still preserving the slavery system within America. Between 1821 and 1867, the Society resettled well over ten thousand African Americans and people of African descent. Its activities ended with the American Civil War, and the group instead focused on education and missionary service. It finally dissolved in 1964.

Pennsylvania, and especially the city of Philadelphia, soon developed into a hub for the gradualist movement. Abolition activities led to the passing of 1780 Gradual Emancipation Act in Pennsylvania, and it was in Philadelphia that free blacks established the first independent black organization and mutual aid society, known as the Free African Society. Two freed men, Richard Allen and Absalom Jones, created this organization especially to serve the needs of Philadelphia's African-American community. By 1790, the society had over two thousand members and was still increasing. In fact, it was Philadelphia that was chosen as the site for the first conference of the American Convention for Promoting the Abolition of Slavery. This Convention brought together several state and regional antislavery societies into a single national organization dedicated to abolition. In the same year, Congress enacted the federal Slave Trade Act of 1794, which prohibited any vessel transporting slaves from **outfitting** in American ports. This meant the slave ships would no longer be able to restock their supplies and find buyers for slaves in US harbors. Finally, on January 1, 1808, the United States outlawed American participation in the African slave trade. The day became an instant holiday for African Americans and the subject of many sermons and celebrations.

Puritans and Quakers were slow to voice reservations as to the morality of the practice, and when protests did begin, they tended to focus on legal arguments rather than ethical ones. Historians now often perceive these protests as lacking the passion of their late-eighteenth- and early-nineteenth-century counterparts. However, it is important to remember these activists did not initially perceive slavery as a cemented evil. During this century, the system of slavery was still fluid, and it appeared more feasible that legal action could prevent the practice from spreading and becoming an unquestioned part of American life. There was a somewhat naive belief that because slavery was so obviously wrong, the general public would not allow the practice to grow and become entrenched. Gradualists were generally perceived as moderates, and most Northerners supported their policy of gradual and compensated emancipation.

Immediatism

Abolition was not initially the name of a movement, but of a section within the movement that disagreed with the gradualists. Known as "immediatism," it denoted a group of radicals who believed in the immediate and complete end of slavery. Many Northern politicians rejected their "extreme" position, including Abraham Lincoln. This group worked in partnership with many free African Americans.

Entering the early eighteenth century, the fight against slavery in America was no longer fought on just a legal battleground. By the end of the 1820s, slavery was a mature and established system, and ninety percent of the black population was enslaved. It was time for new tactics.

This was a period of great change for the abolitionist movement. Transformations in both American political culture and social life had caused the movement to revolutionize. Religious **revivals**, a broader desire for reform, and an emerging free labor market allowed for a new kind of activism—immediatism—to develop and gain wider support.

An elite group who had spearheaded the movement to end slavery from Pennsylvania had given way to a more **egalitarian** movement centralized in Massachusetts. Its equalizing nature both encouraged and responded to the rising prominence of free blacks and female activists within the movement. The group's arguments changed from the legal ones of its political predecessors to new moral and ethical ones. Its tactics focused less on specific legal goals and more on grassroots campaigning and meaningful debates. Immediatists wanted to change not only the country's laws, but the hearts and minds of its people. Perhaps this was because they realized that the law was only as good as the people willing to obey it.

Immediatists differed from gradualists not just in their methods, but in their attitudes. Historian Stanley Harold describes them

Cotton plantations in rural Southern states were heavily reliant on slave labor, unlike the urbanized Northern states.

as "self-righteous, suspicious of compromise, often harsh in their language, capable of violence, and prone to **fatalism**." They are often seen by history as tougher, more violent, and more passionate than the Quaker activists of the gradualist period. Their acts and arguments may not have converted the whole country, but they did push the nation to take drastic steps that would eventually put an end to slavery throughout America.

The North-South Political Divide

It has long been recognized that the Northern and Southern states of America exhibit degrees of difference in their economies, society, customs, and values. By the middle of the nineteenth century, these differences had reached their peak. The North was **urbanized**, prosperous, and largely industrial. Its businesses, factories, and small farms did not need slave labor. Many in the North already believed that slavery was immoral, and between the late-eighteenth and early-nineteenth centuries, Northern states were taking the legal steps required to end the practice.

The South, however, relied on plantation agriculture using slave labor to handle the massive supply orders coming in from Europe and the rest of America. Some Southerners believed that slavery was wrong, but considered it a necessary evil for economic survival. Other Southerners were afraid that the end of slavery would cripple their incomes and end their way of life. Most importantly, many Southerners thought that the federal government had no right to decide whether or not they could own slaves. This attitude was not solely limited to issues of slavery. Before the South began to secede from the Union in 1860, South Carolina had already spoken openly of seceding after the government passed new tax laws in 1832 that the state did not want to comply with. Differences in lifestyle, religious denominations, and political beliefs grew more and more pronounced throughout the 1800s. Northern and Southern **nationalism** were both on the rise with each side vying for the political power that would allow it to dominate the Union.

Beyond the issue of slavery within already established states, there was also the question of the new territories. America was growing rapidly. Year by year new states were becoming part of the country, and it was yet to be decided whether or not slavery would be legal within these new areas. This was not a new problem. As far back as 1787, leading political figures including Thomas Jefferson and James Madison discussed whether or not to include language against slavery in the US Constitution. However, they were anxious to preserve the Union and knew that antislavery measures would likely cause the Southern slave-holding states to secede immediately. In the end, the Founding Fathers decided to bypass the issue, leaving it to be debated and discussed for years to come. They comforted themselves with the knowledge that, at least in 1780, slavery appeared to be on the decline. Northern states were taking steps towards eradication and, in the South, farmers were growing less and less tobacco, further reducing the need for slaves. However, the invention of the cotton gin would soon follow, allowing for a huge increase in demand for slaves, revitalizing the slave market, and changing the political landscape once again.

Harriet Beecher Stowe was born during this tense period of time when Northerners grappled with the ethical dilemmas of the American slave trade and met with Southern resistance.

CHAPTER TWO

Harriet Beecher Stowe: A Life

Harriet Beecher Stowe was born in Litchfield, Connecticut, on June 14, 1811. Christened Harriet Elisabeth Beecher, she was the seventh of thirteen children born to Lyman and Roxana Beecher. She grew up in a simple two-story frame house that was both a family home and a boarding house for scholars from the surrounding community. Harriet grew up during what many contemporaries perceived as Litchfield's "golden age." The Reverend Dan Huntington, Litchfield's pastor from 1789 to 1809, described the town as:

> A delightful village, on a fruitful hill, richly endowed with schools both professional and scientific, with its venerable governors and judges, with its learned lawyers,

Litchfield, Connecticut, provided Harriet Beecher Stowe with access to a more modern and equalized education system than was available in other states at the time.

and senators, and representatives both in the national and state departments, and with a population enlightened and respectable, Litchfield was now in its glory.

Family

Harriet Beecher Stowe's father, Lyman Beecher, was born October 12, 1775. The son and grandson of blacksmiths, Lyman rose to become a Presbyterian minister, cofounder and leader of the American **Temperance** Society, and author of numerous sermons and addresses. He was by nature a passionate and even somewhat fanatical character. He had first entered the ministry at the beginning of a religious revival known as the Second Great Awakening and fervently believed that "the conversion of the world to Christ was near." He studied at Yale Divinity School, graduating in 1797, and was finally ordained in 1799. His yearly salary was just $300, increasing to $400 after five years. This was a meager sum even then, and together the Beechers would later open a private school, where Lyman was a teacher, in order to make ends meet. In her book *Harriet Beecher Stowe: A Life*, scholar Joan D. Hedrick noted:

> His religious zeal … created at home a vortex of paper, books, and ink-blotted notes as well as a residue of moral earnestness and religious **perplexity** that would become for some of his children an almost intolerable burden. His high spirits, warm and impulsive nature, and extraordinary integrity of vision made him a father and husband to be reckoned with.

In his lifetime, Lyman would outlive two wives, get married three times in marriages that would last a total of sixty-two years, and father thirteen children.

Harriet's mother, Roxana Foote, was Lyman's opposite in almost every way. Where he was from a family of traders, she was the granddaughter of General Andrew Ward, who served under George Washington in the Revolutionary War. Where Lyman's education was devoted solely to religion, and he held a deep suspicion of novels and literature, Roxana was highly educated and cultured within her social set. She was fluent in French and considered to be almost a queen within her circle of home-educated girls. Roxana would tie books by the best French authors to her spinning equipment and study as she sat spinning flax. Yet, Roxana was extremely shy outside of her close friendship group. After she and Lyman married in 1799, she struggled with the duties expected of her as a minster's wife. In their first ten years of marriage, she bore him six children, ran the family school in the house, and cared for the student lodgers they took in from the surrounding community.

In addition to this busy and stressful lifestyle, Roxana had to deal with personal tragedy. In 1808, she gave birth to her fifth child, a little girl who she named Harriet after her own sister. When the baby was just one month old, she caught whooping cough. This was a nightly cough that caused convulsive gasping for air. It was particularly dangerous for infants, as they were more likely to wake up choking than gasping. Roxana stayed up night after night watching over the child until finally Lyman insisted she get some sleep. Roxana obeyed, and that night the child died. This would be a source of great sadness for the Beecher family.

When Harriet herself was born three years later, she was given the name Harriet in honor of both her aunt and her deceased sister. Then, in 1816, when Harriet was just five years old, Roxana succumbed to tuberculosis, most likely brought on by exhaustion. Tuberculosis is an infectious lung disease common in the eighteenth century, yet doctors did not yet know what caused it or how to treat sufferers. Roxana was just forty-one years old when she died. Her memory would be deified

The Beecher family was one of the most influential American families of the nineteenth century and was active in many of the key social movements of the period.

by the family for years to come as the perfect submissive image of womanhood. This model would cause Harriet further problems as she took her own first steps into adulthood.

Catherine Beecher was a leading reformer and innovator in women's education.

Harriet had many siblings and half-siblings; however, there were two in particular who were to have a major effect on her life: her sister Catherine and her brother Henry. Catherine was Lyman and Roxana's first-born child and Harriet's oldest sister. Born in 1800, Catherine was an educator and an outspoken supporter of both women's education and the introduction of kindergarten into children's education. She herself was educated at a private school in Litchfield where there was a limited female curriculum that focused mainly on turning young girls into useful wives. As a result of this, Catherine taught herself the subjects that were restricted to male students, such as math, Latin, and philosophy. When her mother died, Catherine was just sixteen and quickly had to take over her mother's domestic duties at home. She became a teacher in 1821. The course of her life changed dramatically, however, when her fiancé, Alexander Fisher, died at sea in 1822. This shocking news was accompanied by the realization that Catherine was not truly prepared for an independent life, having always expected to marry. Her trouble was compounded by her father's insistence that her grief was irreligious and showed a lack of willingness to submit herself to God's will. In 1823, she rallied herself to open her own

The Hartford Female Seminary was set up by Catherine Beecher and would offer Harriet the chance to study subjects traditionally reserved for boys.

school, Hartford Female **Seminary**. Wishing to create a new breed of educational institute for women, Catherine developed her own textbooks in order to deal with the deficiencies of existing ones. She would later move to Cincinnati with her father to campaign for more schools and teachers on the frontier. Her object was "to unite American women in an effort to provide a Christian education for 2,000,000 children in our country."

Brother Henry was born shortly after Harriet and, being the nearest in age, they were very close as children. Henry grew up to become an American Congregationalist clergyman, social reformer, and speaker. He was well known for his support of the abolition of slavery. In the 1870s, Henry was put on trial for adultery. The public attacks on her brother were so painful to Harriet that she moved across the country to escape, yet still asked family to send her updates as the trial unfolded.

Childhood

For most of her childhood, Harriet grew up in Litchfield, Connecticut. After the Revolutionary War, the town had experienced a flowering of theater, women's rights, and education. In many ways, it offered opportunities to young Harriet and her siblings that were not available elsewhere in America at that time. Even within the Beecher house there was a fervent atmosphere of debate and learning. The kitchen table was often the site of academic and religious discussions, in which Lyman would deconstruct ideas and show his children how to create a logical argument. Harriet herself was an avid reader and raised on her prayer book, the Bible, works by Samuel Johnson, and the *Arabian Nights*. Such novels were initially not allowed by her father, who was suspicious of their "**frivolity**," so her uncle Samuel Foote gradually introduced the benefits of such reading. Eventually her father agreed, permitting Walter Scott's novels and Lord Byron's poetry to become staples of discussion at family gatherings. Though the Beechers were a large, mixed-gender family, which gave a rough equality between the siblings, the daughters were not exposed to all the same influences as the sons. Harriet often felt excluded from her brothers' activities and education and was jealous of their lifestyles. She had been raised in a **puritan** tradition that shaped her philosophy of equality and was part of a movement that was determined to fight against social ills like slavery and drunkenness. As a result, Harriet was desperate to make her mark on the world, and this exclusion often made her turn to books and writing for comfort.

Education

At the age of eight, Harriet was allowed to attend the local female academy run by educator Sarah Pierce. Children usually began the academy at twelve; however, she was given a place due to her amazing ability to memorize facts. Lyman spotted Harriet's potential when she was very young but still perceived her gender to be a huge barrier for the age she was living in. He once wrote: "Harriet is a great genius—I would give a hundred dollars if she was a boy & Henry a girl—She is odd—as she is intelligent & studious."

In 1824, Harriet moved to her sister Catherine's school, Hartford Female Seminary. Catherine had founded the institute with the intention of addressing the contrast between the country's republican values and the backward state of female education. At its largest, the school hosted more than one hundred and sixty students, eight teachers, two principals, and a governess—all female. During her time there, Harriet was known to excel when her interests were engaged and to become absent-minded and moody when they were not. She was also observed to be sometimes odd in her manner and habits, but generally a good scholar.

Harriet also later became editor of the school newspaper, the *School Gazette*, where she developed a satirical written style. Her time with the newspaper and the school's focus on essays, at the time not a traditional part of women's education, taught her how to present ideas, adapt concepts, and write in a fluid and interesting manner. Catherine would also often use Harriet to run experiments on the best way to teach traditionally male subjects, such as Latin. This education would prove to be vital training for later life. Harriet was given access to subjects and knowledge previously restricted to boys, and the all-female atmosphere allowed her to present work and opinions in a manner that would have been discouraged in mixed-sex company. In addition, it was during her years at the school that Harriet had her own religious awakening during one of her father's sermons and decided to dedicate her life to Christian values.

Graduation

Harriet graduated from the Hartford Female Seminary in 1827. Almost immediately, she was thrown into a personal crisis. What should she do next? While the school had indeed encouraged the girls to prepare for an independent life, this created its own problems. Hartford provided a female community where boundaries could be pushed and explored; however, the world outside still had very conventional expectations of women. Most careers that would later be seen as acceptable for women were not widely approved by society at the time, such as teaching, missionary work, writing, and activism. In addition, Harriet was conflicted by the memory of her own mother. The timid, saintly Roxana cast a long shadow of "proper womanhood" and did little to provide a model for her fiercely intelligent and independent daughter, who was still looking to change the world. Harriet quickly became seriously depressed. Seeing the change in her sister, Catherine came to the rescue and encouraged Harriet to join her and their father, now living in Cincinnati, to work in social activism.

In 1832, Harriet moved to Cincinnati, Ohio. Her father had become president of the Lane Theological Seminary, while her sister campaigned for the improvement of education on the frontier. At this time, Cincinnati's trade and shipping businesses on the Ohio River were booming. The need for labor had encouraged a huge influx of migrants, including many free blacks and ethnic Irish. The competition for jobs, however, was growing increasingly fierce and, in 1829, riots broke out as Irish migrants attacked black migrants in an effort to push them out of the city. Further riots broke out in both 1836 and 1841, driven by anti-abolitionists.

Living in the city, Harriet witnessed these riots, and the horrors of slavery, firsthand and began reading the abolitionist paper that had sparked these events. Founded by James Birney, who had been a key target during the riots, the *Philanthropist* was a prominent antislavery newspaper in Cincinnati. In her letters to friends and family, Harriet became more and more occupied with the issue, writing: "Pray what is there in Cincinnati to satisfy one whose mind is awakened on this subject? No one can have the system of slavery brought before him without an irrepressible desire to do something, and what is there to be done?" She would later describe her awakening to abolitionism as "a matter of taking the side of the weak against the strong, something the best people have always done."

During her time in Cincinnati, Harriet also joined the Semi-Colon Club, a literary salon and social organization. It was here that she met her future husband, Calvin Ellis Stowe. Other members included future Chief Justice of the Supreme Court Salmon P. Chase, and Judge James Hall, editor of *Western Monthly Magazine*. The group openly encouraged mixed-gender debates and literary activities, and Harriet often presented her early work to the group, although contemporary social standards would have otherwise prevented her from speaking in public to a group that included men. Calvin and Harriet eventually married in 1836 and went on to have seven children together. Like Harriet, Calvin was a passionate critic of slavery and, during their marriage, the couple supported the **Underground Railroad** by temporarily housing fugitive slaves in their home.

Writing

In 1850, Congress passed the Fugitive Slave Law. This prohibited people from assisting fugitive slaves and increased the punishments for such help, even in states where slavery had been made illegal. The law must have struck a chord with both Harriet and her husband. Back in 1839, they had discovered that their own serving maid was in fact a runaway slave and was being hunted by her Kentucky master.

By this time, Harriet, Calvin, and their children had moved to Brunswick, Maine. Calvin taught at Bowdoin College, and the family lived near campus. It was during a communion service at the college chapel that Stowe had a sudden vision of a dying slave and was inspired to write his story. She wrote to the editor of the antislavery newspaper *National Era*, stating that she planned to write a story about the problem of slavery. She wrote: "I feel now that the time is come when even a woman or a child who can speak a word for freedom and humanity is bound to speak ... I hope every woman who can write will not be silent."

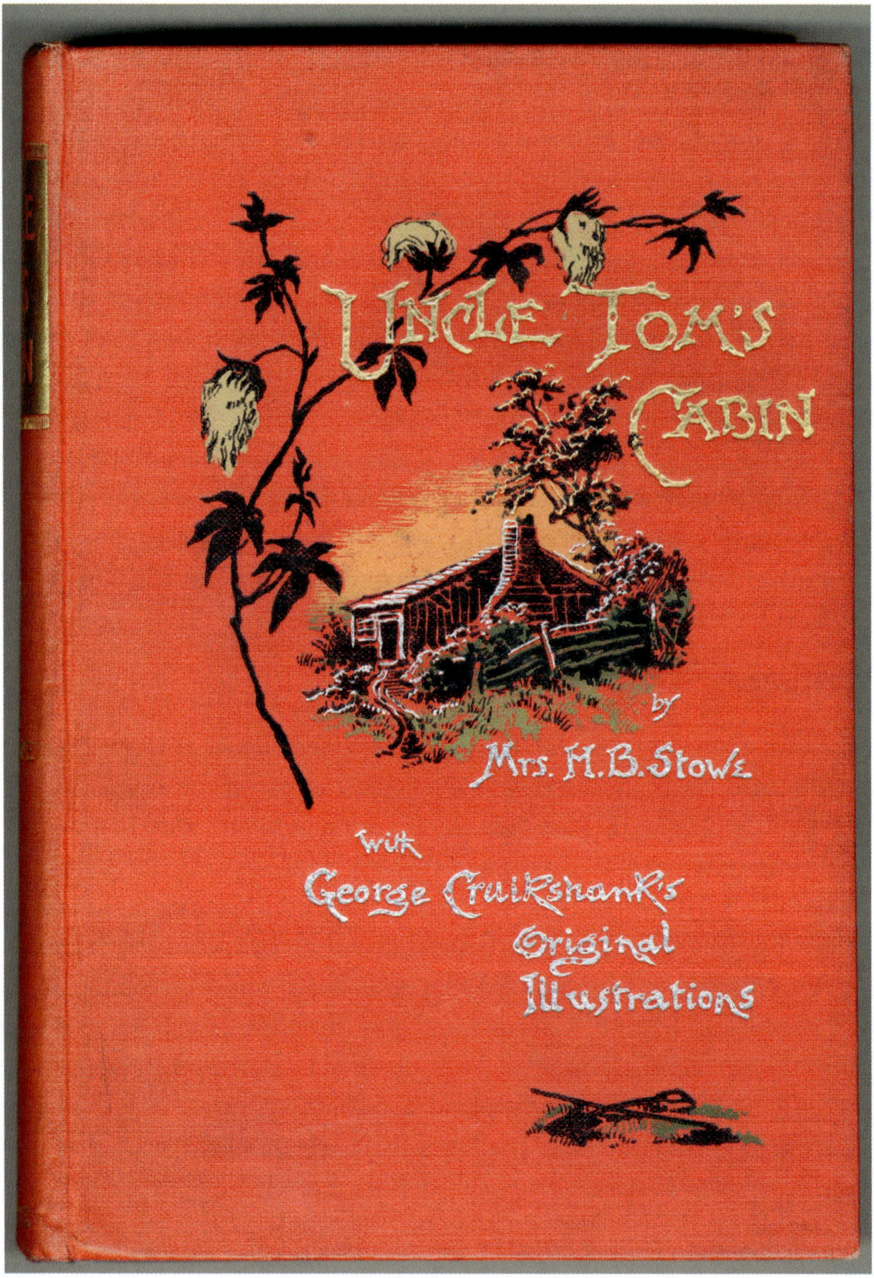

Uncle Tom's Cabin would prove to be the defining work of Harriet Beecher Stowe's life.

The newspaper was quick to commission the story from Harriet. In June 1851, the first installment of *Uncle Tom's Cabin* was released. It ran until April 1, 1852, and Harriet was paid the sum of $400 for her work. Later that year, Stowe published *Uncle Tom's Cabin* as a complete novel with an initial print run of five thousand copies. In less than a year, the book had sold an unprecedented three hundred thousand copies. Despite its success, the book also received heavy criticism from Southern slaveholding states, and many quickly responded with "anti-Tom" novels attempting to portray Southern society and slavery in more positive terms. Many of them actually became best sellers, but none could match the publishing records set by *Uncle Tom's Cabin*. Harriet would later write a literary "key" to the novel in order to tackle criticisms from anti-abolitionist writers and politicians, some of whom had even called her a traitor to her own race.

The popularity of this novel made Harriet an instant celebrity. Soon, she was invited to speak about her novel, slavery, and emancipation in cities across North America and Europe. She was even invited to the White House, where she met President Abraham Lincoln. A legend holds that, upon meeting Harriet in 1862, Lincoln greeted her as "the little woman who wrote the book that made this great war." It is difficult to know whether the president did indeed say this. However, Library of Congress records indicate that Lincoln borrowed her *Key to Uncle Tom's Cabin* that same year.

Before this meeting, Harriet had openly criticized Lincoln for being too slow in abolishing slavery. However, in her memoirs, she would later write:

> Lincoln was a strong man, but his strength was of a peculiar kind; it was not aggressive so much as passive, and among passive things it was like the strength not so much of a stone buttress as of a wire cable. It was strength swaying to every influence, yielding on this side and on that to popular needs, yet tenaciously and

Harriet Beecher Stowe would eventually return to Hartford, where she was buried upon her death in 1896.

believed to have been suffering from **Alzheimer's disease**. Under the watchful eye of her nursemaid, she began to rewrite *Uncle Tom's Cabin*, believing it was for the first time. The *Washington Post* reported at the time:

> She imagined that she was engaged in the original composition, and for several hours every day she industriously used pen and paper, inscribing passages of the book almost exactly word for word. This was done unconsciously from memory, the authoress imagining that she composed the matter as she went along. To her diseased mind the story was brand new and she frequently exhausted herself with labor which she regarded as freshly created.

During this period, author Mark Twain was one of her neighbors in Hartford. He later described her in his autobiography as "always softly slippered and generally full of animal spirits." Her moods were very changeable, and Twain described how she would sometimes "slip up behind a person who was deep in dreams and musings and fetch a war whoop that would jump that person out of his clothes." At other times, according to Twain, she could be found "at the piano singing ancient and melancholy songs with infinitely touching effect."

On July 1, 1896, Harriet Beecher Stowe died in Hartford at the age of eighty-five. She was buried at Phillips Academy in Andover, Massachusetts.

THE BEECHER FAMILY

The Beechers were one of the most influential American families of the nineteenth century. Besides Harriet, Henry, Edward, and Catherine, Lyman and Roxana had seven other children.

William was Lyman and Roxana's oldest son. He was a preacher who believed in abolition, **spiritualism**, and temperance.

Mary was next, but never as political as her family. She partnered with Catherine to open Hartford Seminary but disliked teaching. She would later become grandmother to the writer Charlotte Perkins Gilman.

George was born four years after Mary and eventually studied with the ministry at Yale College. He also became involved in the American Anti-Slavery Society.

Charles was the last child of Lyman and Roxana. He was gifted in languages but loved music. While living in New Orleans, he wrote letters home describing his experiences of slavery that Harriet would later use as inspiration for her novel.

Isabella was the first child of Lyman and his second wife, Harriet Porter. Actively involved in the woman's suffrage movement during the 1860s, she was a founding member of the Connecticut Woman Suffrage Association.

Thomas was born two years after Isabella. Disinterested in the ministry, he was passionate about natural sciences and education. He would later officiate the marriage between Mark Twain and his wife, Olivia Langdon.

James was the third and last child of Lyman and Harriet. He served in the East India trade before moving to China to work as a missionary. He stayed there until the outbreak of the American Civil War.

Lyman Beecher would be hugely influential in the lives of all his children, passing on his religious fervor and zeal, though perhaps not all of his conservatism.

NATIONAL ANTI-SLAVERY STANDARD.

Without Concealment—Without Compromise.

VOLUME 1. NEW-YORK, THURSDAY, JANUARY 7, 1841. NUMBER 31.

PUBLISHED WEEKLY,
BY THE
AMERICAN ANTI-SLAVERY SOCIETY,
AT 143 NASSAU STREET.

NATHANIEL P. ROGERS, Editor.

W. C. ROGERS, General Agent.

☞ To whom Agents, Traveling and Local, will address all letters relating to their agencies.

TERMS—Two Dollars a year, in advance.

Three Dollars if delayed until the end of the year.

Ten Dollars, in advance, will pay for 7 copies one year sent to one address.

Twenty-Five Dollars in advance, will pay for twenty copies one year, sent to one address.

WILLIAM S. DORR, Printer.

SELECTIONS.

The Slave-Trade in Egypt.

LETTER OF DR. MADDEN TO MEHEMET ALI.

ALEXANDRIA, September 6, 1840.

MAY IT PLEASE YOUR HIGHNESS—On the 4th September last I had the honor to lay before your highness an address from the delegates of the Anti-Slavery Convention, recently held in London, expressive of the gratification it afforded that body to learn that your highness, in your late expedition into Africa, had prohibited the crime of man-stealing, and the practice of paying the Egyptian troops stationed in Dongola, Sennaar, and Cordofan, in slaves, a practice which, on the part of your authorities, had hitherto been pursued without let or hinderance.

The communication I had the honor to lay before your highness further expressed an ardent hope that the slave trade, in every place that is subject to your authority, would be entirely prohibited, and the great evil of slavery itself ultimately abolished.

These sentiments and wishes, may it please your highness, are well deserving of consideration, and, even on account of the character of those who have expressed them, are worthy of attention.

The persons who composed that convention (some 400 individuals) were men delegated by bodies of great moral weight and influence in every quarter of the globe, to represent their enlightened and benevolent opinions in that assembly.

They were not selected for the sake of their rank or wealth, but on account of their worth and intelligence, their devotion to the cause of civil, personal, and religious liberty, and the boldness of their maintenance of the interests of humanity wherever they were assailed.

The illustrious man who signed that address, the venerable Clarkson, one whose name is familiar to men's ears in Europe and America as that of an old and faithful friend of the good cause of justice and humanity, is now an aged man, full of years, whom the people of his own country revere and honor, and whose title to the best of all renown is based on the bloodless triumphs of benevolence, on the heroism of his patience and his perseverance in this cause, and the singleness of purpose and simplicity of heart with which he has labored in its service for upwards of fifty years.

The signing of this paper on the part of the venerable man, whose earthly career is now fast drawing to its close, is probably the last public act of his long and useful life; and, subscribed as it is to the expression of sentiments of respect and gratitude for your highness, it may safely be said, without disparagement to the loftiest station or the highest fame, that the greatest of living men might add new lustre to their renown by evincing in their attachment to this cause, and the services rendered to it, that they merited the distinction of receiving from a body of men so justly entitled to respect a similar communication, and one bearing the signature of Thomas Clarkson.

Deputed by that body to communicate these sentiments to your highness, the best token I can give of being in some slight degree deserving of their confidence, is by addressing your highness plainly and unreservedly, without fear or forgetfulness of your authority, or any feeling of distrust in the disposition of your highness to hear the truth, and likewise by distinctly pointing out the glaring evils of this nefarious traffic in human beings, so extensively carried on by your people; and by respectfully but frankly stating to your highness, that the single measure taken at Fezoghan for the repression of this crime on the part of your authorities is utterly insufficient to meet an evil of such magnitude as this.

On the occasion of my presenting the address of the anti-slavery convention to your highness, I observed with feelings of unfeigned satisfaction the interest your highness evidently took in the question of the abolition of the slave trade, and I fully understood that your highness is persuaded of the necessity that exists for the total suppression of it.

While this trade, however, continues (as I am sorry to find it does) to be a source of revenue to your highness, it is in vain to talk of its suppression at Sennaar. I find for each slave sold in the bazaars of Cairo and Alexandria a tax is paid to your highness of one dollar, and on the exportation of each slave another dollar. Independently of these duties levied by your highness on the sale of men, there is a direct permission sold to every gellab to exercise his vile calling, and become a member of the company of slave-dealers, in the same way that the various classes of artisans, bakers, butchers, shoemakers, &c. in Cairo and Alexandria are licensed, and obtain the privileges of a monopoly in the exercise of their respective callings—a license which is called *essendul*, and is given to the gellabs as to any other company legally sanctioned by your highness. It unfortunately happens that it is not in Egypt only, but at Constantinople, and at Smyrna likewise, that this trade in human beings is turned to the account of government, and that a revenue is derived from it. A tax of two-and-a-half per cent. is levied by the Sultan on the sale of every slave, or one para in the piastre of the price of each, on the payment of which tax a paper, called the "penjik," or license, is given to the gellab, and is regarded as evidence of the legality of the sale. Your highness must therefore feel that any application to the mufti at Constantinople, to obtain his consent to the change in the law which I have heard recently suggested, would be preposterous, while the Grand Seignior protects the trade and derives revenue from it.

But I grieve to say that, on inquiring into the nature and extent of the measures which your highness is desirous should be taken to stop this traffic on the part of your officers, nothing whatever has been yet done to give effect to the orders issued for its prevention.

The gratulations of the convention, therefore, on this subject, must apply to the good intentions of your highness towards this cause, and hereafter I earnestly trust it shall be to the effective measures taken to promote its objects in your country that the felicitations of the anti-slavery body shall have to refer.

Since I had the honor of conversing with your highness on this subject, I have visited the slave-markets of Alexandria and Cairo—the former frequently. I have also anxiously inquired into the truth of the reports we have received in England of the cessation of the slave-hunts on the part of your people in the upper country, and consequently of the limitation of slavery, and the hinderance of the trade in slaves.

I have made these inquiries of persons worthy of confidence, of persons who have even recently returned from Sennaar—of those who had actually accompanied your troops in the African slave-hunts; and, expecting to find the trade impeded, the imports diminished, and the markets depressed, I was grieved to find these markets thronged with slaves as heretofore, every notion of decency outraged, as of old, in the centre of your cities; the women in these stalls, in many instances, exposed to the public gaze in a state of nudity, or exhibited to the purchaser with a scanty covering around the loins, or a greasy rug hanging about their shoulders—the unfortunate creatures still subjected to the same cattle-like treatment, to the same exposure and examination of their persons; and moreover, on the authority of the slave-traders themselves, the continuance of the "hunts," and the extension of the ravages of the Egyptian plunderers, on the borders of Abyssinia, still going on.

It was with great surprise that I discovered that the export of negro slaves from Alexandria to Constantinople and Smyrna was still carried on, under the protection of European flags; that one "cargo" of human beings, only a few weeks ago, had been shipped on board an Austrian vessel for Smyrna, and that fraudulent declarations had been allowed to be made, in which the slaves were described as the "servants" of the shipper.

And with no less wonder have I learned that, within the last twelve months, two slave-hunts have been conducted with all the regularity and parade of a large military movement, and not only were connived at, but were actually aided and abetted by the authorities of your highness at Sennaar and its neighboring districts.

An opinion, notwithstanding, had of late become prevalent in England that you had taken such measures for the ultimate abolition of the slave-trade as had already sensibly affected slavery itself, or at least diminished the supply on which that system mainly depended for its continuance. It can hardly be imagined how much error has been disseminated on this subject, amongst a class of persons not much accustomed to be deceived by the apologists of those who sanction slavery, or to give to its terrors the blandishments of an under-stated account of its enormities, and a very exaggerated one of the steps that have been taken for their prevention. Nor will your highness be able very readily to comprehend the extent of our credulity, when you consider only for a moment the crowded state of the slave-markets of Alexandria and Cairo. At the present time there are nearly 200 women and children exposed for sale in the slave-markets of Cairo, and upwards of 100 in that of Alexandria. On the 30th of August, 1840, the following were the numbers in the slave-market of Cairo:—

Abyssinian women,		17
Ditto	boys,	9
Negro	women,	75
Ditto	boys,	90
		191

These returns were obtained from one of the principal gellabs of the slave-market of Cairo; and the following from the general book of registry, kept by the same person, of all the slaves brought from the upper country in the year ending the 31st of August, 1840:—

Abyssinian women,		1700
Ditto	children,	120
Negro	women,	3030
Ditto	children,	270
		5030
Eunuchs,		400
Negro-men of different countries, not brought down to the markets of Cairo and Alexandria, and sold in Sennaar, Darfour, &c.		5000
		10,430

So that the number of negroes captured by your people, in the different slave-hunts during the year ending the 31st of August, 1840, exceeded 10,000!

Now I have positive information, that a large portion of this number were captured by marauding parties, composed chiefly of your soldiers, and consisting of so many as a thousand persons on a single occasion, coming from Sennaar so recently even as 1839; nay, more, that your troops were paid even so lately with the slaves taken in one of these expeditions. My informant, a German naturalist, who was at that period in the service of your highness, and who accompanied your troops on these expeditions, has given me the details at large, and of their fidelity there cannot be the slightest doubt, corroborated as they are by the evidence of other Europeans still in your employment.

This state of things, may it please your highness, and the atrocious mode in which these unfortunate countries are ravaged by your Egyptian and Nubian subjects, the people of England will learn with extreme regret, and the members of the British and Foreign Anti-Slavery Society will lament to find that one solitary act of justice to the negro race, performed by your highness in your expedition to Fezoghan—namely, the liberation of the slaves who were brought to you at that place, and the verbal prohibition of the slave-hunts issued to your officers on that occasion, so far as regarded the payment of your troops with the stolen men—has produced no beneficial effects, and has not been followed up by any other measures of *bona fide* efficacy, that are calculated or intended to put a stop to this abominable trade.

The members of the convention will hear with surprise that at Cartoon, in the vicinity of Sennaar, a French *soi-disant* consular agent, not regularly appointed, but for some years past permitted to retain the title and to exercise the authority he assumed, a man of infamous character—nevertheless recently decorated with the cross of the legion of honor—of the name Vessier, is not only deeply engaged in this odious traffic, but has for some years past been the proprietor of an establishment for the reception and "storage" of slaves, on the plan of "the breeding farms" of Virginia, kept up for the purpose of supplying the Egyptian market with slave children of a tender age. It will be a matter of deep regret, as well as of surprise to that body, to learn that such a miscreant should be suffered to settle in a place under your authority, and that after a formal complaint preferred by the Duke of Wurtemburg to the consul general of the French nation at Alexandria, detailing the enormities of this man in the prosecution of his odious trade, he should still be permitted not only to remain under French protection, but be considered a fit person to be recommended to the especial favor of his sovereign, for a mark of distinction that commonly is, or ought to be, the reward of merit. It may not have reached the ears of your highness, that other foreigners of the same nation were associated with this person in his infamous pursuits; that a Frenchman of the name of Tusot, a physician by profession, till lately living at Cartoon, and who recently resided at Sennaar, was embarked in the same trade, and had attempted the introduction into that place of the practice of making eunuchs, in conjunction with his friend Mons. Vessier, the chevalier of the legion of honor, the slave-dealer of Cartoon.

Your highness was pleased to inform me that the great impediment to the suppression of this trade, or the restriction of slavery itself, was the sanction which the latter received from the law and religion of the land; and therefore, to effect any change, it would be necessary to go to Constantinople, and obtain the concurrence of the head of the religion and the law in any measure that should be proposed for the abolition of slavery, or the trade in slaves.

The fact, I am perfectly aware, is not to be denied, that slavery as it existed of old in the form of domestic servitude, is recognized by the law; but your highness must be well aware that the barbarous wars which are made on the people of Africa for the purpose of obtaining slaves—the perfidy that is practised in entrapping the unwary natives—the violence that is employed in seizing on their defenceless women and children—the murders that are committed in the surprisal of their villages, and the surrounding of their habitations, the starving of their people into terms of submission where they have resisted the marauders, the violation of their women, the capture of the young and the robust, the slaughter of the old and the infirm, the burning of their dwellings, the wasting of their lands—in short, that this savage warfare, and the atrocities that follow in its train, are nowhere prescribed or sanctioned by your law.

It would be a calumny to assert that the religion which is founded on that law is chargeable with the crimes that are committed by the wretches who follow this felonious trade. This trade, may it please your highness, is at variance with every law, human and divine, and the wickedness of it being unknown to the giver of your law, the system that has arisen from it and exists only by its continuance, cannot be considered as that kind of servitude that was tolerated by him, and which had for its object the disposal of prisoners captured in wars undertaken for an aim very different from that of the slave-hunts of Sennaar.

It cannot be denied that it is in the power of your highness to prohibit the crime of stealing men on the part of your people, and the introduction of this species of plunder into the countries over which you rule. A governor without power to enforce its laws, or authority, without the will to curb the violence of lawless men, or protect the weak and the defenceless from their hands, hardly deserves to be respected, and it is hardly to be desired that it should stand.

This evil has been permitted to exist too long for the character of Egyptian civilization. Lesser evils, whose removal was surrounded with greater difficulties, have been encountered and overcome by Mehemet Ali. One of the greatest calamities that the world has experienced during the last three centuries, is that modern barbarity of subduing savage nations to wage wars with one another for the purpose of making slaves. This recent custom of ravaging defenceless nations for an object so unjust and wicked as that of making human beings objects of sale and barter no law can sanction, and no prince can be excused in the sight of God and man who tolerates it on any plea of political or pecuniary advantage.

How, then, may I ask your highness, can it be said that such a trade is lawful, carried on as it is by means of wars that are not just nor necessary, and that the state of the men thus stolen and sold into bondage is so sacred that it cannot be touched, nor even remotely affected, without going to Constantinople, and first asking permission of the mufti to effect some change?

It would be in vain to tell the people of England that the slave trade was to be tolerated in Egypt on the ground of its legality. That plea can only be admitted for its continuance by those who are utterly ignorant of Mohammedan law. It would not be believed that a prince who has the power to triumph over the deepest rooted prejudices of his people, to carry his victorious armies into distant countries, to oppose successfully the greatest obstacles that can be thrown in the way of the accomplishment of his political designs, had not the means at his command of abolishing this trade, and putting an end to the evil practices that have grown out of it.

Amongst these, perhaps, the most barbarous of all is still tolerated, and even encouraged by your highness—the cruel, sanguinary, and most atrocious practice of mutilating men for the purpose of enhancing their value in the market; and, to the disgrace of Egypt, this country still continues to be the only part of the Ottoman empire where it exists.

The civilization of Egypt, may it please your highness, so long as this disgraceful crime is tolerated by your functionaries, and sanctioned by your highness' purchase and employment of the stolen men thus mutilated, for the especial service of your private dwellings—it will be in vain to boast of.

It will be said the only country where this barbarous custom exists, is that which is under the rule of Mehemet Ali. This crime, that is attended with such peril to life, such frightful suffering, such degradation to its victims, is too disgraceful to be permitted in Stamboul; the infamy of it is unknown in Smyrna; in any other part of the dominions of the Sultan it would not be endured; it is only in Egypt that it is suffered, and only there that its profits are a source of revenue to the authorities of the place. Is Europe indeed to be told that the barbarous custom is not to be abolished while Mehemet Ali rules over the land? For nearly five and thirty years he has been its ruler, and he has suffered this evil to exist, and when he is told of the scandal its existence is to his government, is he to entrench the barbarity behind the prohibition of the law, and say, "You must go to Constantinople, because slavery has the sanction of the law"!

Is a custom like this, that slays its hundreds of human creatures every year, that degrades the miserable beings who survive its sufferings in the eyes of their fellow-men, that is sanguinary in its operation, and brutalizing in its influence on the perpetrators of it, to be considered not only a part, but a necessary consequence, of that slavery that has the sanction of law?

If the sanction that is accorded to slavery were to extend to such a crime as this, what a weapon would be placed in the hands of those who were hostile to that law, or whose opinions were regulated by another code!

It is not, please your highness, from the experience of others I speak of this barbarous practice and its effects.—In the year 1826, I was an eye-witness of them at the village of Zawee el Deir, in the district of Sioot. The mortality of the unfortunate children who undergo the operation, by the admission of the wretches who live by the performance of it, was such as could only be credited by persons who have visited the place, and heard the detail of its horrors from the murderous operators themselves.

In the course of fourteen years I find that matters have undergone no change at this place. One of the most devoted of the servants of your highness, Clot Bey, in his recent work on Egypt, states that the practice continues as heretofore, that not much above one fourth part of the children who undergo this operation survive it, and that the number of eunuchs that are made every year is about 300. Some opinion may then be formed of the waste of life that takes place, of the hundreds it is necessary to kill, to have the number that is here given of the survivors of it.

There may be some exaggeration in the account of the mortality given by Clot Bey, but it is still great enough to justify the use of the term 'murderous,' in speaking of this operation. The number of eunuchs made at this place is, however, underrated by him; in the last year the number amounted to four hundred. It is to be borne in mind, that the persons on whom this cruelty is practised are children from the age of six to twelve, and the price for which they are sold varies from one hundred to two hundred dollars.

The operation is performed under circumstances most unfavorable to the safety of those who undergo it. It is performed by ignorant, brutal, and unfeeling men. It is one of a more serious nature than it is generally understood to be. The barbarous application of heated oil, is the medication employed to prevent immediate death from hæmorrhage, and the after treatment, the cruel practice of throwing the unfortunate child on his face in the hot sand, and piling it up about his loins, and then keeping him immoveably fixed in that position for 30 or 40 hours, undergoing torments that cannot be described.

These things, may it please your highness, are done in Egypt.

They are done by Egyptians!
They are done on poor helpless children!
And you are the ruler of the land!

What civilization has reached that land where such savage crimes are committed with impunity!—where they are encouraged by the highest officers of the state, who are compelled by their station to follow the example of your highness, and to surround their doors with a retinue of mutilated men!

In conclusion, may it please your highness, I would beg leave to recall the facts to which I have endeavored to direct your attention.

1. At the expiration of nearly fifteen years I have visited Egypt for the second time, and I find slavery and the trade in slaves unchanged in their character, and unrestrained by any measures of your highness adopted for their suppression.

2. I find the slave markets glutted with negro women and children as heretofore.

3. I find the exportation of slaves from Alexandria for Turkey, on board European vessels, carried on openly at the present time.

4. I find the prices of slaves actually lowered by the increase of the numbers brought down to Alexandria and Cairo, and those slaves, children and women, selling from 600 piastres to 1,300 a-head, or from six pounds sterling to fifteen pounds each.

5. I find the slave hunts are carried on by your people, and even by your soldiers, as usual, and the only prohibition that has been issued, is one given in the presence of certain European consuls at Fezoghan, that never has been carried into effect.

6. I find the same evils arising from this nefarious trade, and the same barbarous monopoly in mutilated beings permitted as heretofore, and even encouraged by your authorities in Upper Egypt.

In the meantime, the spirit of reform is said to be moving over the land; we are told the enlightened views of your highness are directed to the removal of all abuses. Those in the administration of the property of the mosques, which for ages had been protected even by the law itself, were got rid of by your highness without the trouble and inconvenience of going to Constantinople, and the sanction of the law itself was set aside to enable your highness to turn these funds to an account more useful to the state.

But when the grand abuse of all is approached, and the outrages are pointed out that are committed on humanity by the subjects of your highness—when the barbarous traffic in the flesh and blood of human beings like ourselves is brought before you—when the question is not one of rents and revenue, of beans and cotton, but one of flesh and blood, of life and liberty, of duty and of justice, the advocate of the negro must be sent to Constantinople to confer with the mufti about the propriety of any change, because the veneration of your highness for the law is such as to extend even to the shadow of it, under which slavery so tranquilly reposes in those countries that are subject to you.

Your highness did not deem it necessary, when you recently established the national guard at Cairo, to send to the mufti at Stamboul (the head of the religion) to consult him on the investiture of the Sheik el Islam of El Masr (or the chief of the law at Cairo) with the military rank and dignity of a general, and yet the law and the religion had made this man their minister, and the exigency of the times made this minister your soldier. Here the law and the custom of ages were opposed to the change, but the wants of the state, and the will of Mehemet Ali, required that it should be made.

The same will I would fain see exerted in effecting another change, and one that would give the death-blow in Egypt to the crime of stealing men, and retaining these stolen men in slavery. I cannot allow myself to believe this will is wanting on the part of your highness. Other matters, unfortunately considered of greater moment and more immediate political importance, have turned away the attention of your highness from this subject, and afforded you but a single opportunity of manifesting a desire to repress the enormities of this traffic on the part of your military commanders at Fezoghan.

That lesson has been lost for want of repetition. It is not a sudden impulse of generosity, or a single effort of benevolence, that is sufficient to encounter and overcome an evil of such magnitude as that of slavery in any of its forms, but a series of energetic measures, wisely devised and resolutely directed to the abolition of it.

It is idle to pretend that, because slaves are not purchased in Egypt for the purpose of employment in predial labor, and are treated with a degree of humanity little known in Christian countries where slavery prevails, the suppression of the slave trade is not to be desired.

At my recent interview with your highness, in speaking on this subject, you observed that the negroes were in a wretched and distracted state in their own country—that they were perpetually at war with one another, but that in Egypt they were well fed and kindly treated, and were far better off than in their own country; and yet they died by hundreds in the barracks, without any assignable cause after all.

Your highness adduced this fact as a proof of the great difficulty of civilizing the negroes—that after taking them from a state of savage warfare, and making soldiers of them in Egypt, (therefore civilizing them,) they pined away, and they died by hundreds. The civilization, may it please your highness, that is estimated by the advantage of converting an untutored savage into an Egyptian soldier, I do not understand.

As to the negroes being better fed and more humanely treated than in other countries, the injury that was done to them in tearing them from their country surely must have been very great, when so many hundreds of them perished, as you state, without any apparent cause.

The cause of this mortality, may it please your highness, is very intelligible to persons who are well acquainted with the miseries which this traffic is productive of; to those who have some practical knowledge of the sufferings of the negro newly fallen into slavery—of the silent stupor—of the anguish which comes over his mind—of the ties of nature that are broken by his captors—of the throbbings of the heart for house and home of the poor wretch who has been torn from the country (however barbarous it may be) which gave him birth—of the wearing down of his strength and spirits the farther he goes, and the more strongly that he feels "he drags at each remove a lengthening chain."

To assign a cause for this mortality, it is necessary, may it please your highness, to have seen how soon the strongest man sinks under the sense of slavery—how speedily his energies of mind and body are weighed down by it, and how suddenly and silently he pines away in that sickness of the heart which has no hope, except in death.

No matter, however bland and lenient that slavery may be which separates a man from kith and kin—from the place where those nearest and dearest to him lived and died—where the "shieks" and the chiefs of his tribe are buried, and (your highness can well appreciate the force of that local attachment, amounting almost to a religious veneration for the spot) where, perhaps, the bones of his father and mother are likewise laid—you cannot compensate this man for the wrongs he has suffered, except by the restoration of that liberty of which he has been robbed.

But it matters very little, may it please your highness, to the people of Africa, whose country is ravaged, how the captives are treated who are carried away by the Egyptian "gellabs." Whatever the treatment may be in Egypt, the savagery of the war in Africa is all the same. The natives are hunted like wild beasts; their fields are wasted, their villages destroyed, and the defenceless people continually exposed to the marauding attacks of the subjects of your highness.

But, previously to the sale of the slaves in Cairo and Alexandria, nothing that takes place on board the slave-ships of other countries, or in the route of the slave "coffle" in their march across the desert to the coast, can exceed the barbarity with which the gellabs, or slave-traders of Nubia and Egypt, treat the unfortunate captives which they carry from the great emporiums of slavery, Dongola, Darfour, Cartoon, Comomol, and Cordofan.

In their route to Egypt, the wretched slaves are huddled together in small boats on the Nile, in the same way that the wretched negroes are crowded in one dense mass of human beings, jailed and cast down on board the Spanish slave-ships.* It would be idle to expatiate on the sufferings of these creatures during the voyage, or on the hardships they endured in the previous journey over land.

Suffice it to say, on the authority of persons who have very recently even accompanied your soldiers in the slave-hunting expeditions from Senaar, and have returned disgusted from them, that nothing can exceed the barbarity of the usage which the captured negroes experience at the hands of the "gellabs."

But still, with a confident hope in the justice and generosity of your highness, I look forward to the success of this application to your highness, and I most earnestly desire that the sufferings it details may reach your heart. And in the name of humanity itself I appeal to you, on behalf of the poor natives of Africa, whose country your people have hitherto desolated and robbed of its inhabitants, not only with impunity, but even with the sanction of your highness's officers in these distant provinces.

For the grievous wrongs that have been inflicted on the people, the promptest reparation is due to Africa; and, permit me to add, the debt is one which, in justice to yourself, your highness cannot leave unpaid. When that good work which was commenced at Fezoghan, by the liberation of the slaves that were brought before you, shall be accomplished, as I pray it will be by the immediate emancipation of every captive that is brought into your country, the blessings of the poor strangers who have been so cruelly oppressed, and are at length destined to be delivered by you from their sufferings, will then plead for a benefactor, who, in the discharge of the high duties committed to him, had endeavored to do that which was "just and equal to all men."

Such, may it please your highness,
is the humble prayer of
Your highness most ob't serv't,
R. R. MADDEN.

To his highness Mehemet Ali Pacha,
Viceroy of Egypt, Alexandria.

* In the month of December last, three boats of the above description on the Nile, laden with slaves, were seen by Mr. Weir, an English traveller. This gentleman, on whose authority the fullest reliance may be placed, estimates the number on board of each at 150.

From the Dublin Freeman's Journal.

American Slavery.

Mr. John O'Connell alluded, at the last meeting of the Repeal Association, to the fact of the greater portion of the tobacco consumed by the people of Ireland being the produce of slave labor; and we had great pleasure in hearing the honorable member—after detailing some of the horrible atrocities perpetrated by the American slave owners—call upon his fellow countrymen to renounce the use of an article obtained at the expense of blood, and which may be truly said to be 'watered by the tears and moistened by the sighs of groaning wretches.' We trust and hope—now that the Irish people have been made aware of the cruelties to which the cultivation of this noxious weed subjects the unfortunate negroes of the southern States—that a feeling of indignation sufficiently strong to lead to its disuse will take possession of the public mind, and that the men who are seeking for the restoration of national rights at home, will be among the first to strike at the root of the abominable system which recognises and confesses the right of property in human beings abroad. An excellent letter on the subject, from the pen of our philanthropic fellow-citizen, Mr. James Haughton, will be found in another part of this morning's paper.

LETTER TO THE IRISH PEOPLE,

On the use of articles produced by the labor of slaves, particularly tobacco.

I am induced on the present occasion to address a few words to my countrymen, by a conversation which I had lately with a few of them among the humbler classes of society, on the subject of the use of tobacco. The persons I allude to expressed such an anxious desire, and begged of me so earnestly to give the people some information relative to the production of that article and some other things in general use, which are produced by slave labor in America and some of the West India Islands, that I feel induced thus to give public expression to some ideas that have occupied my mind since I was in London, in June last, at the Anti-Slavery Convention. It affords me peculiar pleasure that I am urged on by men of humble rank to call the attention of all classes of society to the important topic to which I have alluded—*to the use of articles which are the produce of slave labor.* I feel myself quite incompetent to do justice to this great subject, but I venture to bring it before the minds of my countrymen, in the hope that some gifted individuals, some persons more acquainted with the subject than I am, may come forward and devote their talents to this holy cause. I shall not therefore enlarge on the question at present, but shall merely open it, and leave it with the public for further consideration and the discussion of its merits. My object is to strike at the root of slavery by urging the propriety of giving up the use of all articles which are produced by slave labor, that is, by the labor of men, women and children liable to be bought and sold like cattle, and who are compelled to work by the whip. Tobacco is one of these articles, and as it is a mere useless luxury, I feel a conviction, amounting almost to a certainty, in my mind, that my countrymen will at once give up its use, and relinquish any gratification it may afford them, when they are informed that it is cultivated by slaves, such as I have above described—by men, and women too, who are their fellow-creatures, created by the same gracious God, with similar feelings, and having the same high hopes of a glorious immortality—when they are informed that these beings are held as we hold cattle, by white men who pay them no wages, and who frequently flog them in such an inhuman manner, that it is literally true that their blood manures the tobacco, rice, and cotton which they toil to raise for our gratification. My countrymen and friends, you will not, I hope, continue to feed the plundering white man—who, while he is acting in this unjust and savage manner, dares to call himself a Christian—by supplying him with the means to continue his hellish traffic in the bones and sinews of his brother, and to live in luxury on the unrequited and coerced toil of his victim. You support this wicked system by the use of tobacco; it is at best a useless luxury. I believe it to be injurious to man's health; but, at all events, give it up, cast it from you with loathing and disgust, so long as it is saturated with blood. If it be an innocent luxury, which I do not believe it is, let us have it by innocent and lawful means; let the American and Cuban planters set their brethren free, let them pay them fair wages for their labor; then, and then only, can we consent to deal with them, if we would keep a 'conscience void of offence towards God and man.' We must push forward the great and glorious work of universal emancipation; it has received a fresh impulse, and our labors must not cease until the work is accomplished. I said that I was urged to write this address by a few individuals of humble rank, and that this circumstance afforded me peculiar pleasure; it does so, because it assures me that my countrymen have, within a short period of time, made great progress in religious and moral feeling. In this simple circumstance I behold some of the glorious results of the temperance reformation, which first made them rational, then reflecting, and now, I trust, benevolent human beings. If I am permitted, I shall, in a future letter, state my opinions relative to the use of cotton goods; and endeavor to show that, by encouraging the use of linen instead, we would confer a benefit on our own country, and assist in destroying the hideous vice of slavery in America. I shall conclude for the present by stating that my hopes of success depend more on the cooperation of the poor than of the rich. I behold the former rushing forward in hundreds of thousands to shake off the vice of drunkenness; such a noble determination on their part assures me that they will relinquish willingly another bad habit, when they are informed that the sacrifice will evince their sympathy for their black brethren who are held in cruel bondage. That the rich may also awake, and become zealous in the cause of humanity, is the sincere prayer of my heart. In any case, the work of human improvement must go forward. Like the seed which has lain dormant within the rock, but which opens into life after the slumber of ages when it is placed in a proper soil, and called into being under the genial influence of the sun, so the germ of humanity in our hearts, called into activity by the cheering beams of charity and benevolence, will spread its branches over the earth. Let all who believe in God hasten to usher in this blessed day. The press will lend its powerful assistance in breaking the chains of slavery, and letting the oppressed go free.

It is hoped that all persons who approve of the foregoing sentiments, will give them as much publicity as possible. It is well to diffuse good principles, both through the press and by means of social intercourse.

JAMES HAUGHTON.

Dublin, Oct. 1840.

From the Philanthropist.

The Black Code of Ohio.

This week we devote a large portion of our paper to an exposition of the Black Code of Ohio. Most of what follows we wrote in the winter of 1838–9, but it will not be out of place now, when all eyes are directed to the Assembly in hopes of a reform in our legislation.

DEGENERACY.

This is the year eighteen hundred and forty. That religion, which breathes peace on earth and good will to man, and commands us to do unto others as we would they should do unto us, made its advent nearly nineteen centuries ago. The blessings imparted by its presence, who can tell? Despotism has been smitten by its power, and is now crumbling in decay. Civil liberty has sprung up to its footsteps. Under its influence slavery has ceased to exist in the British dependencies. France and every other nation, save our own, under the same influence, are about severing the chains on human limbs. In some of the states of this Union, the march of liberty has been steadily onward. Massachusetts, Vermont, and New York have protested against the gag-resolutions of Congress, and spread the broad ægis of a jury trial over the personal liberty of all within their borders. Sixty-four years ago, our fathers, moved by the free spirit of Christianity, solemnly proclaimed the grand doctrines of human rights. Thirty-eight years ago, the free settlers of Ohio, the framers of our Constitution, affirmed the same great doctrines, and fixed the brand of their reprobation forever on the spirit and practice of slavery.

Within a few years past, in full view of these glorious effects of Christianity, the sons of these settlers, the descendants of the revolutionary fathers; men, who call themselves christians; republicans, who scoff at the servile spirit and sentiments of *monarchies*; with the lights of Christianity beaming upon them, the voice of mercy pleading against them, their professions of superior devotion to freedom staring them in the face; spurning every feeling dear to our common humanity, forgetful of the contempt with which posterity will regard their memories; in violation of the constitution they were sworn to maintain; in disregard of the rights of the people they were sworn to protect; in contempt of the eternal, unchangeable principles of truth and justice, and in defiance of God—have bowed down before the demon of slavery, and, in obedience to its demands and the exactions of an iron prejudice, trodden upon the weak, forged chains for the best affections of the human heart, and enacted laws to uphold and perpetuate a stupendous system of violence, robbery and licentiousness.

TIMES BEFORE THE CONSTITUTION.

Before the formation of our present constitution, under the territorial form of government, no distinction was ever recognised in Ohio, between the rights of white persons, and the rights of free colored persons, except in a single point. By a law of 1799, all but white persons were exempted, or rather excluded, from service in the militia. In all other respects, the rule of equality was universal. In the convention that framed our constitution, the question of depriving the colored people of the right of suffrage, gave rise to much discussion. At first, a majority of the members was in favor of continuing to them this right; for, on motion to insert a clause to secure this privilege to all males residing in the territory, the vote stood, yeas, 19; nays, 15—every member being present. "A motion to extend the same privilege to their descendants was lost by a vote of 17 to 16, one member being absent. On the third reading of the article, a motion was made to strike out the clause which had been previously inserted, extending this privilege to persons of color as above stated, which was carried by the casting vote of the president, on tie of all the members. On the question of striking out a clause which had been inserted, excluding them from giving testimony in courts of justice against white persons, it was carried in the affirmative, by a vote of seventeen to sixteen, one member absent."*

These votes of the Convention show, how far the framers of the constitution intended to restrict the rights of colored people.

But the example of oppression had been set, and subsequent legislation gave evidence of its corrupting tendencies. The spirit of slavery demanded heavier impositions on the people of color, and the demand was obeyed. We here insert the two Acts of Ohio, in relation to "Blacks and Mulattoes," passed 1804 and 1807. Let every man, who has one sentiment of humanity or equity in his bosom, after the examination of these laws, say, whether they ought longer to remain on the statute book.

AN ACT to regulate Black and Mulatto persons.

SEC. 1. *Be it enacted by the General Assembly of the State of Ohio.* That from and after the first day of June next, no black or mulatto person shall be permitted to settle or reside in this State, unless he or she shall first produce a fair certificate from some court within the U. States, of his or her actual freedom; which certificate shall be attested by the clerk of said court, and the seal thereof annexed thereto by the said clerk.

SEC. 2. That every black or mulatto person residing within this State, on or before the first day of June, one thousand eight hundred and four, shall enter his or her name together with the name or names of his or her children, in the clerk's office, in the county in which he, she or they reside, which shall be entered on record by said clerk; and thereafter the clerk's certificate of such record, shall be sufficient evidence of his, her or their freedom; and for every entry and certificate, the person obtaining the same shall pay to the clerk, twelve and a half cents: *Provided nevertheless*, that nothing in this act contained, shall bar the lawful claim to any black or mulatto person.

SEC. 3. That no person or persons residents of this State, shall be permitted to hire, or in any way employ, any black or mulatto person, unless such black or mulatto person shall have one of the certificates as aforesaid, under pain of forfeiting and paying any sum not less than ten, nor more than fifty dollars at the discretion of the court, for every such offence, and one half thereof for the use of the informer, and the other half for the use of the State; and shall moreover pay to the owner, if any there be, of such black or mulatto person, the sum of fifty cents for every day, he, she or they shall in any wise employ, harbor or secrete such black or mulatto person; which sum or sums shall be recoverable before any court having cognizance thereof.

SEC. 4. That if any person or persons shall harbor or secrete any black or mulatto person, the property of any person whatever, or shall in any wise hinder or prevent the lawful owner or owners from retaking and possessing his or her black or mulatto servant or servants, he or they shall, upon conviction thereof, by indictment or information, be fined in any sum not less than ten, nor more than fifty dollars, at the discretion of the court; one half thereof for the use of the informer, and the other half for the use of the State.

SEC. 5. That every black or mulatto person who shall come to reside in this State, with such certificate as is required in the first section of this act, shall within two years, have the same recorded in the clerk's office, in the county in which he, or she means to reside, for which he or she shall pay to the clerk twelve and a half cents; and the clerk shall give him or her a certificate of such record.

SEC. 6. That in case any person or persons, his or their agent or agents, claiming any black or mulatto person or persons, that now are, or hereafter may be, in this State, may apply upon making satisfactory proof that such black or mulatto person or persons is the property of him or her who applies to any associate judge or justice of the peace within this State, the associate judge or justice is hereby empowered and, required by his precept, to direct the sheriff or constable to arrest such black or mulatto person or persons, and deliver the same, in the county or township where such officers shall reside, to the claimant or claimants or his or their agent or agents; for which service, the sheriff or constable shall receive such compensation as they are entitled to receive in other cases, for similar services.

SEC. 7. That any person or persons who shall attempt to remove, or shall remove from this State, or who shall aid and assist in removing contrary to the provisions of this act, any black or mulatto person or persons, without first proving as herein before directed, that he, she or they is, or are legally entitled to do so, shall, on conviction thereof before any court having cognizance of the same, forfeit and pay the sum of one thousand dollars; one half to the use of the informer, and the other half to the use of the State; to be recovered by action of debt, qui tam, or indictment; and shall moreover be liable to the action of the party injured.

ELIAS LANGHAM,
Speaker of the House of Representatives.

NATHANIEL MASSIE,
Speaker of the Senate.

January 5th, 1804.

AN ACT to amend the last named Act.

SEC. 1. *Be it enacted by the General Assembly of the State of Ohio.* That no negro or mulatto person shall be permitted to emigrate into, and settle within this State, unless such negro or mulatto person shall, within twenty days thereafter, enter into bond with two or more freehold sureties, in the penal sum of five hundred dollars, before the clerk of the court of common pleas of the county in which such negro or mulatto may wish to reside, (to be approved of by the clerk,) conditioned for the good behavior of such negro or mulatto, and moreover to pay for the support of such person, in case he, she or they shall thereafter be found within any township in this State, unable to support themselves; and if any negro or mulatto person shall emigrate into this State, and not comply with the provisions of this act, it shall be the duty of the overseers of the poor of the township where such negro or mulatto may be found, to remove immediately such black or mulatto person, in the same manner as is required in the case of paupers.

SEC. 2. That it shall be the duty of the clerk before whom such bond may be given as aforesaid, to file the same in his office, and give a certificate thereof to such negro or mulatto person; and the said clerk shall be entitled to receive the sum of one dollar for the bond and certificate aforesaid, on the delivery of the certificate.

SEC. 3. That if any person, being a resident of this State, shall employ, harbor or conceal any such negro or mulatto person aforesaid, contrary to the provisions of the first section of this act; any person so offending, shall forfeit and pay for every such offence, any sum not exceeding one hundred dollars, the one half to the informer, and the other half for the use of the poor of the township in which such person may reside; to be recovered by action of debt, before any court having competent jurisdiction; and moreover be liable for the maintenance and support of such negro or mulatto, provided he, she or they, shall become unable to support themselves.

SEC. 4. That no black or mulatto person or persons shall hereafter be permitted to be sworn or give evidence in any court of record, or elsewhere, in this State, in any cause pending, or matter of controversy, where either party to the same is a white person; or in any prosecution which shall be instituted in behalf of this State, against any white person.

SEC. 5. That so much of the act entitled "An act to regulate black and mulatto persons," as is contrary to this act, together with the sixth section thereof, be and the same is hereby repealed.

This act shall take effect and be in force from and after the first day of April next.

ABRAHAM SHEPHERD,
Speaker of the House of Representatives.

THOMAS KIRKER,
Speaker of the Senate.

January 25th, 1807.

Without any comment at this time on the section relating to freedom certificates, we remark, that the law in regard to testimony, is founded on the assumption, that colored people do not appreciate the obligations of truth, or of an oath. It is a standing libel on their character, branding them all, in effect, as LIARS. Its tendency certainly is, to degrade them in their own estimation, take off from their conduct the powerful check of self-respect, tempt them to demoralizing tricks to secure rights which no just law throws open to villainous encroachment, and check their industry and keep down their spirit of enterprise, by rendering of uncertain acquisition the rewards of honest labor. While it operates thus upon the colored man, it offers occasion to unprincipled white men to gratify their avarice or resentment at the expense of the former. Need we here speak of the fraud and violence to which colored people are continually subject? It were almost a work of supererogation. The observation of perhaps every member of the Assembly can furnish facts bearing on this point. Let them call to mind the case of Scott's murderers—a wife, prohibited from giving testimony that might lead to the detection of her own husband's assassin! The persons arrested are awaiting their trial; but many a heart troubles with apprehension lest justice should yet be defrauded of its claims, by the law which the Assembly is now called on to repeal.

Take another case which took place not many years ago in this State, a case related to us by the lamented Charles Hammond, who often in conversation with us, expressed his hostility to this law.

A white man and a colored man quarrelled. The former became angry, drew his knife, and his antagonist sought safety in flight. The white man pursued him, followed him into his house, and cornered him. It was too dark to discern objects distinctly. The little son of the colored man was lying in the corner whither his father had retreated, when, awakened by the noise, he started up in front of him. That moment, the knife of the white man, blind with rage, entered his bowels, almost laying bare the whole cavity. The child died. The murderer left the house and kept his own counsel; none had witnessed the deed but the family and a few colored inmates, and *justice never could be had*, the murderer went unpunished, for a colored man's oath was inadmissible! The law is entirely gratuitous. Every white man, who is not gangrened by prejudice, *knows*, that the character of the colored people in this State generally, is such as to make them credible witnesses. Besides, why call in question the competency of a jury of twelve men of common sense to decide on the credibility of testimony? This they do in the case of white witnesses. Why not let colored evidence go to them on the same condition? The law is as absurd as it is wicked, and the Christianity of the people of Ohio demands its repeal.

SCHOOL LAW.

But the spirit of slavery was not yet satisfied. The degradation of the colored man was not complete. So long as one privilege above his bare natural rights was accorded to him, the slaveholder had ground for offence, and his friends in this State were discontented. The colored man was still entitled to participate in the benefits of the common school fund. He could still educate his children, and thus cherish the hope that their intelligence might one day secure to them privileges from which he was cut off. But this hope was crushed. A free colored population, enlightened and virtuous, is a thorn in the flesh of the slaveholder. "Let there be darkness!" was his decree, and it was obeyed. The colored man was shut out from the benefits of the common school, and doomed to mental as well as civil degradation.

Before the organization of our State government, the Congress of the United States passed a law, in which was incorporated the following proposition for the acceptance or rejection of the Territory of Ohio: "That the section number sixteen in every township—and, where such section has been sold, granted, or disposed of, other lands equivalent thereto, and most contiguous to the same—shall be granted to the inhabitants of such township for the use of schools." The only condition annexed was, that the "State would, by an irrevocable ordinance, exempt the lands of the United States from taxation for the term of 5 years from and after the day of the sale." "The State of Ohio in convention assembled, accepted the above proposition on condition 'that all the lands before mentioned, to be appropriated by the United States to the support of schools, shall be vested in the Legislature of this State, in trust for said purpose.'" Congress agreed to this modification of the former proposition, and the grant was accordingly made.

Such were the circumstances attending this grant. No conditions were annexed, no phraseology employed, which could authorize the supposition, that it was the intention of Congress to exclude from the benefits of these donations the colored children of the territory. Let us now see whether the framers of the Constitution intended thus to limit the benefits of schools endowed in whole or in part from the revenue arising from these lands.

Sect. 25th, Art. VIII. of the Constitution declares—

"That no law shall be passed to prevent the poor in the several counties and townships within the State, from an equal participation in the schools, academies, colleges, and universities within this State, which are endowed, in whole or in part, from the revenue arising from the donations made by the United States for the support of schools and colleges; and the doors of the said schools, academies, and universities, shall be open for the reception of scholars, students, and teachers of every grade, without any distinction or preference whatever, contrary to the intent for which the said donations were made."

The language of this provision is full and explicit. It leaves nothing to conjecture. It secures to the poor of "every grade," colored as well as white, the benefit of the common school fund. The correctness of this construction is confirmed by the uniform practice of the State, from the date of the adoption of the constitution down to 1829, a period of twenty-seven years. That year, for the first time, the legislature violated this provision of the constitution, by depriving colored children of the privilege of attending the common school. In 1831, another act was passed, "An act to provide for the support and better regulation of common schools;" in which it is provided, "That a fund shall hereafter be raised in the several counties of this State, in the manner pointed out by this act, for the use of common schools, for the instruction of the white youth of every class and grade, without distinction, in reading, writing and arithmetic, and other necessary branches of education." By the same act, the property of "Blacks and Mulattoes," was exempted from taxation for school purposes; howbeit, it is a fact, that from that time to the present, this exemption generally has existed only on the statute book, their property having been annually taxed, for the support of schools, from which their children have been excluded.*

The school laws passed since then, retain these obnoxious provisions. Petitions are now probably before the legislature, praying such modification of them, as at least to entitle colored people to a fair proportion of the proceeds of donations made by the United States for school purposes; and it would be hard to say, why the prayer should not be granted. [illegible] they constitute a quiet, orderly, useful class of the community—it certainly is for the interest of all, that they should have every proper facility granted them for the improvement of themselves in knowledge and virtue.

A LEGAL SETTLEMENT AND THE RIGHT OF JURY-TRIAL.

To fill up the cup of our iniquity, we have denied to the colored man the privilege of obtaining a "legal settlement," in the State. This is a grievance, hard to bear. [illegible] it is well known, that paupers among the colored people of Ohio are rare, and the few there be, [illegible] supplied by those of their own color.

* Judge King's Report.

* Some three sessions ago, a movement was made looking towards justice—but so far as we know, it has not succeeded.

it was discovered Stowe had used the narrative as a major source for her work, its sales increased dramatically. Henson would even rename later editions *An Autobiography of the Rev. Josiah Henson (Mrs. Harriet Beecher Stowe's "Uncle Tom")*, and use the larger proceeds from the book's sales for his school and community.

Theodore Weld and the Grimké Sisters

Another major influence on Stowe, as well as many who lived in antebellum America, was *American Slavery As It Is: Testimony of a Thousand Witnesses*. Authored by Theodore Weld, his wife Angelina, and her sister Sarah, the book was published in 1839 and contained firsthand accounts from slaves of their daily lives. It focused on many aspects of slavery, from diet and clothing to housing and working conditions. It also discussed and analyzed several proslavery arguments to reveal their logical and humanitarian flaws. The work was distributed by the American Anti-Slavery Society and was later seen as the second most influential piece of antislavery literature of the period, second only to *Uncle Tom's Cabin*.

Theodore Weld and several other students quit Lane Theological Seminary, where Harriet Beecher Stowe's own father was headmaster, due to the establishment's pro-colonization views.

Though the authors themselves had never been slaves, they were heavily involved in the abolition movement. Theodore Weld was a white New Englander and had dedicated himself to the abolitionist cause in 1830, after leaving the university he attended due to its stance on slavery. He was one of the founding members of the American Anti-Slavery Society. In 1836, the Society decided to dedicate its resources toward enlarging their band of trained lecturers, whose job it was to spread abolitionist ideas amongst the public. This new class of lecturers was called the Band of Seventy. They were trained in New York and included Sarah Grimké and her sister, Weld's future wife, Angelina Grimké. Throughout his time as a campaigner, Weld was known to speak for eight to ten hours a day, but he was forced to end his speaking career in 1836 due to the strain. He continued to work for the American Anti-Slavery Society as an editor for several of their publications and acted as an aid to antislavery members of Congress.

Angelina and Sarah Grimké were originally raised as Southerners but spent their entire adult lives living in the North. They were both abolitionists, women's rights advocates, and writers. Despite their Quaker convictions, they did not shy away from the threat of violence. Two years after joining the Band of Seventy, Angelina gave a speech in Philadelphia and triumphed, despite having a hostile crowd shouting and throwing stones outside the hall the entire time. Both sisters would later be very active in the Massachusetts Woman Suffrage Association in the 1870s. Speaking on the subject of abolition and women's rights, Angelina Grimké once said: "Women ought to feel a peculiar sympathy in the colored man's wrong, for, like him, she has been accused of mental inferiority, and denied the privileges of a liberal education."

Antislavery Rhetoric

Harriet Beecher Stowe was not only influenced by the wider world around her, but by her private life as well. Her family played an integral part in forming her political identity, though she did not always follow their beliefs. Her father had shaped her religious convictions and her oratory style, and her sister had shaped many of her political inclinations. Her brothers, too, provided key models for civic behavior.

Sarah Grimké was active in both the abolition and women's rights movements.

Edward Beecher shared Harriet Beecher Stowe's political beliefs and helped to inspire her actions in speaking out against slavery.

Edward and Isabella Beecher

Stowe's brother Edward was a noted **theologian** of the period. He had entered Yale at just fifteen and worked his way through college by teaching, graduating finally as class valedictorian. Like Stowe, he had been influenced by their father's religious zeal; however, he was much more liberal than Lyman Beecher. Edward was an advocate for abolition, the immediate end of slavery and racial inequality, rather than his father's choice of colonization (transporting slaves back to Africa). Edward was great friends with the antislavery advocate and reverend Elijah Lovejoy. After Lovejoy's violent death at the hands of a proslavery mob, Beecher wrote a broad indictment of slavery and mob violence. He firmly believed that all of America was responsible for slavery, since the entirety of white society profited from it.

In the spring of 1850, Stowe's husband Calvin was offered a job at Bowdoin College, and Stowe traveled through Boston, staying with her brother and his wife for a week. It was the same year as the second Fugitive Slave Act was due to be made into law, and Edward and Isabella openly discussed and raged against it. Later that year, when the act did indeed pass, Isabella wrote to Stowe saying: "[I]f I could use a pen as you can, I would write something that would make this whole nation feel what an accursed thing slavery is." Harriet responded to her sister-in-law by vowing, "I will write something. I will if I live."

Sentimental Culture and Republican Motherhood

Sentimentality and "sentiment" were a major part of nineteenth century culture. Sentimental culture valued the use of heightened emotions, empathy, and the ability to be moved. During this time, the sign of a truly cultured and intelligent person was their ability to be emotionally affected by others. *Uncle Tom's Cabin* was specifically designed to appeal to this desire and to the conflicted emotions

ABOLITIONIST LITERATURE

During the 1800s, one of the easiest ways for abolitionists to spread their ideas was through publishing articles in newspapers and magazines. Dedicated antislavery newspapers and magazines cropped up throughout this period, including the *Emancipator* (1819–1820), the *Philanthropist* (1836–1837), and the *National Anti-Slavery Standard* (1840–1870). Three particularly important antislavery newspapers were the *Liberator*, the *Slave's Friend*, and the *National Era*.

William Lloyd Garrison and Isaac Knapp founded the *Liberator* in 1831. Garrison had previously worked for the *Emancipator* but left largely due to his belief in abolition rather than gradualism. While the paper had a circulation of only three thousand during its lifetime, it gained notoriety for its unwavering advocacy of immediate abolition. It ran for three decades until the ratification of the Thirteen Amendment, which abolished slavery throughout the United States.

The *Slave's Friend* was a children's antislavery magazine produced by the American Anti-Slavery Society. It aimed to teach children tolerance and to equate slavery with sinfulness. One article even sought to clamp down on racist language with instructions such as "Never … call a colored man a BOY. This is often done, and it is insulting and foolish."

The *National Era* was an abolitionist paper published weekly in Washington, DC. Beginning in 1847, its aim was "a complete discussion of the Question of Slavery and … the Duties of the Citizen in relation to it." It later published *Uncle Tom's Cabin* in a serialized form before it was published as a novel.

Newspapers were a critical tool of the abolition movement, helping to disseminate information and protest throughout America and rallying new supporters to the cause.

of nineteenth-century America, divided as it was over the issue of slavery. Stowe crafted her language to make her readers feel the suffering and injustice of slavery, rather than offering philosophical or legal arguments against it. She specifically used techniques of sentimental fiction to show the devastating effects of slavery on family life. The aim of the narrative was to compel every reader on an emotional level to fight against this system of inequality.

It is easy to underestimate how incredible the power Stowe held was. In a time where women could not speak publicly without **reprisals**, she fought to speak her mind on issues close to her heart. Sentimental culture, especially for women, was closely tied with American society's vision of how women should act. During Stowe's time, women were not expected to speak out in public, but were instead expected to tend to their domestic responsibilities and raise their children. Stowe rebelled against this attitude toward women and, in speaking out against the ills of slavery, fought against the American notion of "Republican motherhood."

"Republican motherhood" is the twentieth-century term for an attitude towards women's roles in the United States before, during, and after the American Revolution. The period lasted roughly from 1654 to 1920. It centered on the belief that the daughters of patriots should be raised to uphold the ideals of **republicanism**, in order to pass on these values to the next generation. The "Republican mother" was seen to be a custodian of civic virtue and responsible for upholding the morality of her husband and children. This weighty title was a mixed blessing. On the one hand, it encouraged the education of women and gave the traditionally female sphere of the home a dignity and importance that had previously been missing. On the other, it also reinforced the idea of a domestic women's sphere separate from the public world of men.

But Stowe lived during a time when this traditional idea of women's roles was beginning to change, albeit slowly. During the 1800s, a more gender-equalized education system created an influx

"Republican" mothers bore a heavy duty of being morally responsible for their families, while having very little power to affect change without their husbands' permission.

of white, middle-class women into public life. Scholar Mary Kelley describes this phenomenon as follows: "Many women educated at these schools began to press the boundaries that had limited a female's engagement with public life, calling for equal access to the social and cultural domains that had been the preserve of men." One of Stowe's contemporaries was Margaret Fuller, a journalist, critic, and women's rights advocate. She spoke in favor of the movement claiming: "We would have every path laid open to women as freely as to men." However, it was not easy for most women to move their interests and voices into the public sphere and, rather than fight for their own rights, women became more and more involved in the abolition movement. Stowe is one of the most famous examples of this, although many other women would become influential in the abolitionist and, later, women's rights movements.

This new generation of women decided to take the moral authority that Republican motherhood granted them and push it outwards into the world, declaring that the public sphere itself was simply another home—the house of God, in fact—and so they were perfectly within their rights to bring moral order to its inhabitants.

UNCLE TOM'S CABIN
ELIZA'S ESCAPE

CHAPTER FOUR

Uncle Tom's Cabin

Harriet Beecher Stowe was a prolific writer. Over a career spanning fifty-one years, she published thirty books and countless short stories, articles, and hymns. She wrote everything from children's textbooks to homemaking and childbirth guides, biographies, and religious studies. She was intensely interested in contemporary political issues, and her writing was a political act. It allowed her to express her thoughts and beliefs at a time when women could not speak out publicly.

But it was her most famous work, *Uncle Tom's Cabin*, which made her a household name. Published in 1852, the novel sold three hundred thousand copies in the United States and one million copies in the United Kingdom within its first year. It was the bestselling book of the nineteenth century, second only to the Bible. However, it remains to this day a

Eliza's "flight across the ice" became one of the book's most iconic scenes and was replicated in hundreds of theater shows, novels, and artworks.

controversial work. Its supporters have credited it with helping the abolitionist cause during the 1850s, and some still believe it to be one of the most successful feats of persuasion in American history. Others are not so convinced. Critics have damned *Uncle Tom's Cabin* for its popularization of a number of black stereotypes: the affectionate, dark-skinned mammy; the black child as pickaninny; the dutiful slave loyal to white masters; and the desirable mulatto woman.

Several key events conspired to finally bring *Uncle Tom's Cabin* to life. The book was written largely in response to the passage of the second Fugitive Slave Act in 1850, but there were other contributing factors. Stowe composed the tale in Brunswick, Maine, where her husband was teaching at Bowdoin College. In 1849, her son Samuel died at eighteen months due to a cholera epidemic. Her still-raw grief had led her to fixate more and more on Jesus Christ and Christ-like figures, which she had begun to explore in her literature. She would later say that losing her child had helped her to understand "what a poor slave mother may feel when her child is torn away from her."

In February 1851, while attending mass at the college's chapel, Stowe had a vision of an old slave being whipped by two fellow slaves, who were goaded on by a brutal white man. Stowe was inspired to tell this slave's story, and the narrative would eventually become *Uncle Tom's Cabin*. She wrote to publisher Gamaliel Bailey of the Washington-based antislavery newspaper *National Era* to offer him the story, and he quickly contracted her to compose a tale that would "paint a word picture of slavery." The first installment was released in June 1851, and over the next forty-one weeks, Stowe made it her goal to educate Northerners on the horrors of slavery and to create empathy. Inspired by the recent publishing increase in slave autobiographies and by the many tales she had heard from friends and fugitive slaves, she structured the tale around relatable individuals who would show how slavery affected all sections of society.

Scenes from slave narratives, such as the sale of family members and loved ones, helped Harriet Beecher Stowe to create more realistic scenes and characters.

Plot, Style, and Structure

The novel follows the narratives of two Kentucky slaves, Tom and Eliza. Their owner, Arthur Shelby, has a large amount of debts and decides to sell Tom to a slave trader. The trader, Mr. Hadley, also insists on buying Eliza's son, Harry. Eliza learns of this plan and warns Tom, before fleeing the plantation with her child. As she heads north, Tom is sold down the Mississippi River. While on board the boat taking him south, he meets a young white girl called Eva. He saves her life after she falls overboard, and her father, Augustine St. Clare, buys Tom from the slave trader. Tom remains with the St. Clare family until Augustine's death, when he is sold to the villainous Simon Legree. Life on the Legree plantation exposes Tom and the reader to the worst possible circumstances of slavery. Angered by Tom's piety, Legree beats Tom viciously in an attempt to break his spirit. While on the plantation, Tom meets two slave women named Cassy and Emmeline. In the novel's final scene, Tom helps Cassy and Emmeline escape and, as a result, is whipped to death by Legree's overseers. Even as he lies dying, Tom forgives his tormentors, refusing to allow Legree to destroy his faith.

Uncle Tom's Cabin is written in the sentimental and **melodramatic** style common to nineteenth-century fiction. This genre tended to feature a central female character and a writing style designed to evoke a reader's sympathy and emotion. While Stowe borrowed heavily from the tradition of melodramatic writing and sentimental culture, she also adapted it for her purpose. She focused on the larger political theme of slavery, rather than the politics of the home, and used a man as the main character. Her adaptation of the style was extremely successful and often caused very strong reactions in her readers. Her friend, Georgina May, wrote to Stowe:

> I sat up last night long after one o'clock, reading and finishing 'Uncle Tom's Cabin.' I could not leave it any more than I could have left a dying child ... I thought I

> was a through-going abolitionist before, but your book has awakened so strong a feeling of indignation and compassion, that I seem never to have had any feeling on this subject till now.

Another facet that made Stowe's writing so powerful was the religious influence of her upbringing. She wanted to preach on paper as her brothers were doing at that time in the pulpit. What made her brothers' sermons so effective was their narrative preaching style, turning a moral lesson into a story. Through this, Stowe realized how much more effective narrative was for persuasion than speeches. As a result, throughout the novel, her authorial voice often steps back from the narrative to furnish scenes with a direct heartfelt appeal to the reader's own experience and emotions.

The story is structured in two parallel plot lines: the Northern plot with Eliza, and the Southern with Tom. While Stowe took pains not to demonize all Southerners nor praise all Northerners, there is a clear contrast between Tom's "descent" into the South and the corresponding worsening of his conditions, and Eliza's "ascent" north toward Canada and her increasing freedom and happiness. The tale itself exploded the myth of the **paternalistic** South, attacking the image of the white Southern patriarch by showing how slavery broke up families and how even "kind" masters showed a lack of care and "Christian love" to slaves.

Themes

The key theme of the novel is the evil of slavery in response to the second Fugitive Slave Act of 1850. Stowe primarily used a story in order to explore this theme, but really she delivered a skilled argument advocating for the immediate emancipation of slaves and freedom for all people. She was attempting to break down all the popular defenses of slavery, especially paternalism and the "moral and mental inferiority" of African Americans. She created a story

Harriet Beecher Stowe wanted her work to break down idealized depictions of slave life and expose the grinding inhumanity of the practice.

that incorporated examples of slavery under the "best" conditions, with humane masters such as Augustine St. Clare, to its very worst ramifications, including sexual exploitation, physical abuse, and the tearing apart of families. Stowe was not trying to suggest that slavery could be pardoned through "better" masters, but instead to highlight how there were no conditions that would make life as a slave tolerable or be in the best interests of an enslaved individual. This directly attacked a common contemporary defense of slavery that stated that most masters acted in their slaves' best interests. Stowe wanted to refute this by showing that the slave's best interest could lie only in obtaining freedom.

The novel travels from the Shelby plantation to the St. Clare plantation and finishes at the Legree plantation. The first two-thirds of the narrative are set in the "mild" conditions of the Shelby and St. Clare plantations, where slaves are not abused or mistreated. Both owners, Arthur Shelby and Augustine St. Clare, show kindness and intelligence, but their ability to tolerate slavery for monetary gain makes them hypocritical and weak. The struggling Arthur Shelby sells Tom to repay his debts, destroying Tom's family in the process. Marie St. Clare sells Tom again after the death of Augustine despite her husband's promise to free Tom. After undermining the argument for slavery as protection, Stowe then moves the reader to Legree's plantation to shock her readers out of complacence. The moment Tom arrives there, the pleasant veneer is broken. Legree's plantation is a harsh and barbaric setting where beatings, sexual abuse, and murder occur. This is the final stage of Stowe's persuasive argument: If slavery is wrong in the "best" of circumstances, then it is nightmarish and inhuman at its worst.

The Power of Women

Women hold a key position within the narrative. They are the underpinning force for social change. Stowe firmly believed that women had the moral authority to save the United States from the "demon" of slavery. Female characters within the book are often held up as examples of morality and the power of morality against evil practices.

Eva St. Clare is presented as the ideal Christian and the most moral white character in the tale. Her piety and selflessness help her to positively influence those with more power than her. Although she is a child, she is a driving force for morality in the novel.

Eliza escapes slavery to save her son; it is her need to protect him that gives her the courage and strength to escape her pursuers, and it is she who reunites her entire family at the end of the novel. Stowe describes Eliza, upon learning her son will be sold, as follows: "It is impossible to conceive of a human creature more wholly desolate and forlorn than Eliza, when she turned her footsteps from Uncle Tom's cabin … But stronger than all was maternal love, wrought into a paroxysm of frenzy by the near approach of a fearful danger." This facet is particularly important. Stowe presented slavery as a force that broke families apart, and maternal love is shown in the end to be the force that can heal this fracture.

Similarly, Stowe explores the consequences when women are ignored or left powerless by their husbands. When Tom is first sold, Arthur Shelby's wife, Emily, desperately tries to change his mind. He refuses and, as she has no legal power over their property without his consent, she cannot prevent the transaction. However, Emily plays a larger role than just Shelby's emotional wife. She is the guardian of her husband's soul and the welfare of others. Emily desperately tries to prevent her husband from committing an act she knows to be morally wrong, which places him at risk of refusal to Heaven. Stowe notes that "Mrs. Shelby was a woman of high class, both intellectually and morally" while Arthur Shelby "seemed somehow or other to fancy that his wife has piety and benevolence enough for two—to indulge a shadowy expectation of getting into heaven through her superabundance of qualities to which he made no particular pretension." As Shelby damns Tom, he also damns himself. His wife recognizes this and has the moral strength to attempt to dissuade him.

Uncle Tom's Cabin sought to reaffirm the importance of women's influence, and some say it paved the way for the women's rights movement in the following decades. Conversely, some critics have argued that Stowe's female characters were more often domestic clichés rather than realistic women. Some have stated that these women are more often than not one-dimensional stereotypes: submissive, pure and angelic, or vain, silly, and self-centered.

Christianity

Uncle Tom's Cabin is usually defined as an antislavery narrative, but it is also clearly part of a long tradition of Christian literature. In Stowe's mind, abolition and Christianity walked hand in hand. It was her belief that Christian theology was fundamentally incompatible with slavery, meaning that if all people practiced universal Christian love, then it would be impossible for one group to oppress another. While Stowe uses the narrative to emphasize the evil and destructive nature of slavery, she also parallels this with the assertion that Christian love can overcome this destruction.

Within the narrative, the more religious a character is, the more they object to slavery. Eva, the most moral white character, fails to understand why the adults around her see a difference between black and white people. Legree, on the other hand, is a professed atheist and practices slavery almost as a method of deliberate blasphemy and evil. Similarly, religion is used as a tool to redeem immoral characters within the narrative. When slave hunter Tom Loker is injured and then spared by slaves and healed by Quakers, he learns his lesson and becomes a changed man.

Main Characters

Uncle Tom

Uncle Tom is a noble and long-suffering slave. He is the central character around whom the other characters' stories revolve. Throughout the novel, he experiences many trials, but he consistently stands up for his beliefs and is even grudgingly admired by his enemies. However, history has not been kind to Uncle Tom, and his name has become an epithet for African Americans who are accused of "selling out" to whites. More specifically, to call someone an "Uncle Tom" means that he or she is like an old black man eager to please his white masters and happy to accept a position of inferiority. This meaning has most likely evolved from what some see as Tom's passivity. Critics have argued that Tom's passive acceptance is insulting because it is so at odds with the resolve and strength of modern civil rights crusaders.

Yet, the modern perception of an "Uncle Tom" is not entirely true to the novel. First, Tom is not particularly old. At the beginning of the book, we are told that Tom is eight years older than Arthur

time she has actually spent with black people has made her find them uncomfortably alien, and she avoids letting Topsy touch her.

Miss Ophelia is an obvious surrogate for Stowe's intended audience, almost as if she has brought one of her own readers into the narrative. Stowe takes pains to show that much of Ophelia's prejudice comes from unfamiliarity and ignorance, rather than actual experience-based dislike. When Ophelia first meets Topsy, she acts only out of duty and displays a clear dislike for the child. However, through Eva's death, she connects to Topsy on an emotional level and comes to love Topsy as a human being. She finally overcomes her prejudice and provides a model to Stowe's Northern readership.

Evangeline St. Clare

Evangeline, better known as Eva, is the young daughter of Augustine St. Clare. She meets Tom on the steamship to New Orleans, and he saves her life after she falls overboard. She is portrayed as the most Christian white character and spends most of the narrative talking of love and forgiveness. Before dying, she gives a lock of her hair to all of her father's slaves and tells them to become Christians so they can see each other again in Heaven. On her deathbed, she makes her father promise to free Tom; however, this promise never materializes due to Augustine's sudden death.

CHAPTER FIVE

Contemporary Reactions

On August 26, 1852, the Honorable Charles Sumner of Massachusetts gave a speech in the United States Senate on his motion to repeal the Fugitive Slave Act:

> A woman, inspired by Christian genius … and with marvellous power sweeps the chords of the popular heart. Now melting to tears, and now inspiring to rage, her work everywhere touches the conscience … in a brief period, nearly 100,000 copies of *Uncle Tom's Cabin* have been already circulated. But this extraordinary and sudden success … cannot be regarded merely as the triumph of genius. Higher far than this, it is the testimony of the people, by an unprecedented act, against the Fugitive Slave Bill.

The fame of *Uncle Tom's Cabin* soon reached the heights of the US Senate and became intertwined with antislavery rhetoric.

This inspired woman was no less than Harriet Beecher Stowe herself. Within less than a year, *Uncle Tom's Cabin* had gained such an iconic position within contemporary culture that it could be referenced in the midst of a crucial Senate debate. This gives some idea of the scale of the success and notoriety Stowe and her novel gained within a relatively short period of time. The novel's contemporary supporters hailed it both as a masterpiece and a political force of nature. However, despite its commercial and cultural success, *Uncle Tom's Cabin* was a problematic and controversial novel from the moment of its publication. To fully understand the breadth and depth of contemporary reactions to Stowe and her work, we must examine not only different perspectives within America, but also across the wider world. *Uncle Tom's Cabin* was a global phenomenon that did not only affect the United States. In fact, it is possible to find opinions ranging from the academic critic to the emotional public in almost every country that was touched by the Atlantic slave trade.

Positive Reactions

Uncle Tom's Cabin was a great success with a large majority of the public. In the United States, the book became the first widely-read political novel and massively influenced both American literature and protest literature in general. It would later inspire works such as *The Jungle* by Upton Sinclair and *Silent Spring* by Rachel Carson—twentieth-century books that protested social and environmental issues. Stowe's work also found high praise in Canada. With the country's strong ties to community projects begun by self-emancipated people and individuals who had migrated north, Stowe found a ready audience in her Canadian readers.

A Global Response

Stowe's work also traveled across the Atlantic to find readership in the United Kingdom. Stowe herself was in communication with numerous famous British writers and pro-abolition politicians, including Charles Dickens. One critic described a gathering where Stowe had traveled to England for a reading tour:

> There was a degree of excitement in the room that can better be imagined than described. The waving of hats and handkerchiefs, the clapping of hands, the stamping of feet, and the screaming and fainting of ladies, went on as if it had been in the programme, while the thieves were at work helping themselves out of the abundance of the pockets of those who were most crowded.

However, interest in the novel wasn't always generated from solely selfless reasons. One English contemporary of Stowe's noted:

> The evil passions which Uncle Tom gratified in England were not hatred or vengeance [of slavery], but national jealousy and national vanity. We have long been smarting under the conceit of America—we are tired of hearing her boast that she is the freest and the most enlightened country that the world has ever seen. Our clergy hate her voluntary system—our Tories hate her democrats—our Whigs hate her parvenus—our Radicals hate her litigiousness, her insolence, and her ambition. All parties hailed Mrs. Stowe as a revolter from the enemy.

In the wider world, the novel soon gathered force among foreign readers. By 1857, *Uncle Tom's Cabin* had been translated into twenty different languages and was later translated into almost every major language, including Chinese.

However, it is important to remember that not all readers approached the novel from the same position. While white readers had the luxury of maintaining a certain distance from the text, the first African-American communities to contend with *Uncle Tom* did

Frederick Douglass was a famous intellectual and reformer, as well as a leading figure of the antislavery movement.

so in the context of a fully-matured slavery system, strengthened proslavery legislation, and controversial plans to expand slavery to the territories.

The Critics

Uncle Tom's Cabin has long had a complicated relationship with its critics but, for the most part, the work received very positive reviews from contemporaries. It was credited with focusing Northern anger at the injustices of slavery and the Fugitive Slave Law, and away from fretting about whether one state had the jurisdiction to ignore the edicts of another. One Union general and politician, James Baird Weaver, stated that the book had convinced him to become active in the abolition movement.

Many African-American critics were equally effusive in their praise of Stowe and her work. One such critic was Frederick Douglass, a social reformer, abolitionist, orator, writer, and statesman. During his lifetime he published an abolitionist newspaper called the *Frederick Douglass Paper*, in which a review of *Uncle Tom's Cabin* was printed in April 1852. The author is believed to have been either Douglass or his colleague Julia Griffiths. In the article, the writer claimed that "[t]he friends of freedom owe the Authoress a large debt of gratitude for this essential service rendered by her to the cause they love." The power of the novel to change hearts and minds was also highlighted as the writer described how "the touching portraiture [Stowe] has given of 'poor Uncle Tom,' will, of itself, enlist the kindly sympathies, of numbers, in behalf of the oppressed African race, and will raise up a host of enemies against the fearful system of slavery."

On May 20, 1852, another review of *Uncle Tom's Cabin* was published in the *Frederick Douglass Paper*, written by William G. Allen, stating:

> I have recently read 'Uncle Tom.' What a book! It is, in its line, the wonder of wonders. How its descriptions stir the blood, indeed almost make it leap out of the heart! What declinations of characters-St. Clare and Legree, extremes of slaveholders. While the latter is a fit representative of the system of the pit, the former shows that not even slaveholding itself can blot out every whit of whatsoever is good in the human heart. Thank God for this little space wherein one vivifying ray may enter!

As can be seen in both these reviews, pro-abolitionist critics were particularly concerned with swaying public sentiment and believed that it was through the power of the masses that slavery would be ended.

Another African-American writer who was deeply affected by Stowe's work was Frances Harper. Born Frances Ellen Watkins, Harper was a poet and author active in social reform and a member of the Women's Christian Temperance Union, which itself advocated progressive social reform. After reading *Uncle Tom's Cabin*, she published a four-stanza poem in the *Frederick Douglass Paper* in which she thanked Stowe for "thy pleading / For the fettered and the dumb, … the kindly words / That gree'd thy pen of fire / And thrilled upon the living chords / Of many a heart's deep lyre." Harper praised Stowe's ability to change hearts and minds and, like other pro-abolitionist critics, focused on emotions rather than the logical arguments used by Stowe's Quaker predecessors. Harper would continue to be influenced by the novel in her later works, writing literary tributes to characters like Eliza and other slave mothers.

Across the Atlantic in England, African-American critics living in exile also commented and debated on Stowe's novel. After the passing of the 1850 Fugitive Slave Law, many freed slaves spent time overseas for several years due to the increased risk of capture and re-enslavement. One such intellectual was William Wells Brown, an abolitionist lecturer, novelist, playwright and historian. Born into slavery in Montgomery County, Kentucky, Brown had escaped to Ohio at the age of twenty. Brown spent years as a free man, working on the waterfronts in Cleveland and Buffalo, learning to read and write, and becoming increasingly involved with the antislavery movement. After publishing his own autobiography, *Narrative of William W. Brown, a Fugitive Slave*, he attended the 1849 Peace Congress in Paris before traveling to England. He was lecturing in England when the 1850 law was passed, and he decided to stay in the country for the next four years. Later, when his freedom was purchased in 1854 by a British couple, Wells and his two daughters returned to the United States. Reviewing the novel for the American abolitionist paper the *Liberator*, Wells claimed that: "Uncle Tom's Cabin has come down upon the dark abodes of slavery like morning sunlight, unfolding to view its enormities in a manner which has fastened all eyes upon the "peculiar situation," and awakening sympathy in hearts that never before felt for the slave."

In Canada, African-American critics also made themselves heard. Henry Bibb was the child of a white Kentucky senator and an enslaved women named Mildred Jackson. As a young man, Bibb tried on numerous occasions to escape from the plantation on which he was enslaved. This was due largely to his own enslaved wife being forced into sexual relations with her master. His sense of outrage and helplessness grew to fever pitch, and after he had facilitated his escape, Bibb eventually became a powerful antislavery lecturer. He worked alongside Frederick Douglass and William Wells Brown, as well as Josiah Henson, to found the Refugees Home Colony in Canada. In addition, he was the founding editor of Canada's first African-American newspaper, the *Voice of the Fugitive*. The paper was instrumental in creating more national sympathy for black people in Canada. It was in this publication that Bibb printed commentaries on *Uncle Tom's Cabin*, as well as real-life accounts of captures and confrontations that emphasized the truthfulness of the horrors within the novel. Bibb was also not afraid to verbally attack critics who disparaged Stowe's criticisms of slaveholder behavior.

Henry Bibb was best known for his establishment of the abolitionist paper *Voice of the Fugitive.* The paper published slave narratives, antislavery articles, and reviews of both pro- and antislavery literature.

One writer from the *Christian Observer* complained of Stowe that "People who 'live in glass houses ought not to throw stones' … [whether] it not be well for us to turn our thoughts inward and see how we ourselves stand in the sight of God, before we accuse our Southern neighbors of hypocrisy?"

Bibb hit back with biting sarcasm:

> We presume, as the above remarks are from a paper entitled "*Christian* Observer," that the writer either imagines himself to be a Christian, or wishes to pass himself off as such: the latter is, in all probability, the true state of the case. We would like to know what description of slavery that is which so far perverts the intellect as to cause a man to imagine that an endeavor to reform abuses—a wish to make men do to each other as they would have others do to them—is "quarrelling with our Maker." What does the writer mean? Are we to understand that all the systems of villainy now established in the world are under the direct patronage of the Divinity, and that they are not to be interfered with until the Divine Power sees fit to remove them? If this is indeed a fact, how egregiously men have erred in all times past! Rejoice, ye housebreakers and midnight assassins—let the whole fraternity of criminals rejoice—for your time honored vocations are under the protection of God! Society has no right to interfere with your peculiar employments; and the appointment of magistrates, police and penitentiaries for the purpose of arresting you in your infernal occupations, are only so many implements of war directed against the Divine Power, which permits and protects your existence.

Essentially, Bibb mocked the writer in his suggestion that the lifestyles and institutions of nineteenth-century life were decreed by God and thus should not be interfered with. He further skewers this viewpoint by sarcastically suggesting that if this was the case then logically crime and criminals themselves must also be divinely permitted.

Negative Reactions

As has been previously discussed, *Uncle Tom's Cabin* provoked outrage in the South. Some were angered by what they perceived to be an untrue or exaggerated depiction of slavery; others were insulted by the "hypocrisy" of a Northern public who profited by the system of slavery but distanced itself from the reality. A bookseller in Mobile, Alabama, was forced to leave town for even selling the novel. Beyond the South, the book was heavily criticized by slavery supporters with some going so far as to claim Stowe was a traitor to her race. The anger became so vitriolic that Stowe received numerous threatening letters. One package actually contained a slave's severed ear.

The Critics

Proslavery critics were equally strong in their reproofs, lining up to claim that the novel was utterly false, criminal, and scandalous. Immediately after its publication, they set about attacking Stowe's credibility as an accurate portrayer of the slave's condition. They took pains to highlight Stowe's lack of experience in the South and the fact she had never been on a plantation. Despite Stowe's rebuttals that her scenes and characters were taken from real-life slave accounts, critics continued to claim that she could not possibly create accurate descriptions of the region.

Only a few months after the release of *Uncle Tom's Cabin*, Harriet Beecher Stowe found herself under vicious attack from Southern writer Louisa S. McCord of the *Southern Quarterly Review*. McCord wrote: "Mrs. Stowe, in spite of experience, in spite of science, determines that the negro is intellectually the white man's equal …

admitted to Harvard Medical School, but who were later dismissed due to complaints from a group of white students. Most historians believed him to have been the first proponent of black nationalism. This was a movement that advocated for economic self-sufficiency, racial pride for African Americans, and black separatism. Delany firmly believed that Stowe portrayed slaves as too passive, though he praised her pointed emphasis on the cruelty of Southern slave owners. Over time, Delany became more convinced that only black people could advance their own cause and interests. He was not alone. Historian Lois Brown has argued that many African Americans, both at the time of the novel and since, have perceived Stowe's novel as fundamentally missing the point of portraying black experience, noting:

> While some may have read the novel in order to gain insights into African-American identity or about American culture, history, and race relations, *Uncle Tom's Cabin* may have functioned more deliberately as a handbook on how to be white in America.

There were two other areas of concern. First, some African-American critics did not fully support Stowe's depictions of the South, believing them to be somewhat ham-fisted. Even Henry Bibb admitted in one review that the novel "partakes somewhat of caricature of Southern habits and Southern Christians" and has the unflattering "habit of some people at the North to call into question the sincerity of those professors of religion, who happen to live in a slave-holding state." Secondly, Stowe's decision to transport Eliza and her family back to Liberia at the novel's end essentially advocated for the colonization of black people—a movement most African Americans vehemently opposed. In private, Frederick Douglass wrote to Stowe, stating: "Madam, we are Americans. We are not going back to Africa. Though I like your book, I don't like this part of your book."

THE AMERICAN ANTI-SLAVERY SOCIETY

The American Anti-Slavery Society, also known as the AASS, was an abolitionist society that began in 1833 and ran until 1870. Founded by activists William Lloyd Garrison and Arthur Tappan, the society reached a membership of roughly 250,000 at its height and established 1,360 local chapters. Notable members included Susan B. Anthony, Elizabeth Cady Stanton, Theodore Dwight Weld, Lydia Maria Child, and John Greenleaf Whittier. Black statesman Frederick Douglass was a key leader, and activist William Wells Brown often spoke at society meetings. The organization was headquartered in New York, where they created and distributed several antislavery publications including the *National Anti-Slavery Standard*. The AASS was largely perceived as controversial and sometimes met with violence when mobs invaded meetings, attacked speakers, and burned printing presses.

TWENTY-NINTH ANNIVERSARY

OF THE

American Anti-Slavery Society,

Tuesday, May 12, 1863.

I.

C. M.—MARLOW.

1. The land our Fathers left to us
Is foul with hateful sin;
When shall, O Lord, this sorrow end,
And hope and joy begin?

2. What good, though growing might and wealth
Shall stretch from shore to shore,
If thus the fatal poison-taint
Be only spread the more?

3. Wipe out, O God, the nation's sin,
Then swell the nation's power;
But build not high our yearning hopes,
To wither in an hour!

4. No outward show nor favored strength
From thy stern justice saves;
There is no liberty for them
Who make their brethren slaves!

II.

6s and 4s—ITALIAN HYMN.

1. Ye who in bondage pine,
Shut out from light divine,
Bereft of hope;
Whose limbs are worn with chains,
Whose tears bedew our plains,
Whose blood our glory stains,
In gloom who grope:—

2. Shout! for the hour draws nigh
That gives you liberty!
And from the dust,
So long your vile embrace,
Uprising, take your place
Among earth's noblest race—
'Tis right and just!

3. The night—the long, long night
Of infamy and slight,
Shame and disgrace,
And slavery worse than e'er
Rome's serfs were doomed to bear,
Bloody beyond compare—
Recedes apace!

4. Lorn Africa, once more,
As proudly as of yore,
Shall yet be seen
Foremost of all the earth
In learning, beauty, worth—
By dignity of birth
A peerless Queen!

5. Speed, speed the hour, O Lord!
Speak! and, at thy dread word,
Fetters shall fall
From every limb—the strong
No more the weak shall wrong,
But Liberty's sweet song
Be sung by all.

III.

BATTLE HYMN OF THE REPUBLIC.

Mine eyes have seen the glory of the coming of the Lord:
He is trampling out the vintage where the grapes of wrath are stored:
He hath loosed the fateful lightning of his terrible swift sword:
His truth is marching on.

Chorus—Glory, glory, hallelujah, etc.

I have seen him in the watch-fires of a hundred circling camps;
They have builded him an altar in the evening dews and damps;
I can read his righteous sentence by the dim and flaring lamps:
His day is marching on.

Chorus—Glory, glory, hallelujah, etc.

I have read a fiery gospel writ in burnished rows of steel;
"As ye deal with my contemners, so with you my grace shall deal;
Let the hero, born of woman, crush the serpent with his heel,
Since God is marching on."

Chorus—Glory, glory, hallelujah, etc.

He has sounded forth the trumpet that shall never call retreat:
He is sifting out the hearts of men before his judgment-seat:
Oh, be swift, my soul, to answer him! be jubilant, my feet!
Our God is marching on.

Chorus—Glory, glory, hallelujah, etc.

In the beauty of the lilies Christ was born across the sea,
With a glory in his bosom that transfigures you and me;
As he died to make men holy, let us die to make men free,
While God is marching on.

Chorus—Glory, glory, hallelujah, etc.

IV.

L. M.—OLD HUNDRED.

1. From all that dwell below the skies,
Let the Creator's praise arise!
Let the Redeemer's name be sung,
Through every land, by every tongue!

2. Eternal are thy mercies, Lord!
Eternal truth attends thy word!
Thy praise shall sound from shore to shore,
Till suns shall rise and set no more!

1399 Frais & Co.'s Steam Print, 11 Frankfort St. (near City Hall), N. Y.

The American Anti-Slavery Society was one of the most famous organizations of the abolition movement. Many of its members would go on to be leading figures in future movements, such as women's rights.

LA BELLE RIVIERE

CHAPTER SIX

Stowe's Lasting Influence

The influence of Harriet Beecher Stowe is undeniable but problematic. Her most famous work, *Uncle Tom's Cabin*, holds an uneasy place in American race and protest literature. Critics have spoken out with a huge range of opinions but, in more recent times, these have been largely negative. The black American poet Langston Hughes described the novel as "the most cussed and discussed book of its time." British novelist George Orwell called it "the best bad book" of its period. Even today, in classrooms and lecture halls across the world, modern students often feel embarrassed by the book. They cringe at Stowe's language and portrayals, even as they recognize the importance of the novel in American history and in the wider "race conversation" that the country has been engaged in for hundreds of years.

The 1965 film adaptation of *Uncle Tom's Cabin* attempted to reframe the character of Tom and redress previous criticism of the character.

However, Stowe is not entirely to blame here. A large part of the bad reputation the book has garnered happened through its misappropriation by others. Writers, critics, and artists, both modern and contemporary, have left indelible marks upon the novel. In the wake of the novel's contemporary success, theatrical adaptations and minstrel shows sprang up and adapted the story for their own needs. Characters were reduced to one-dimensional objects, symbolism was drowned out by show tunes, and religion was replaced by extreme sentimentality. Once her characters were in the public eye, there was very little Stowe could do to control how and when they were used. In the words of critic Hollis Robbins: "Uncle Tom began as a Christ figure—a character like Jesus who loves God, loves his tormentors, turns the other cheek, and shows inhuman forbearance in the face of cruelty—but has been transformed into the perfect, silver-haired, silent, sexless, stalwart servant."

Is *Uncle Tom's Cabin* Still Relevant Today?

Stowe's work, both her novel and her wider political activism, discusses themes and issues that are still relevant today. Black rights, the representation of one race by another, women's rights, and the place of women's fiction in the literary canon are as significant now as they were in Stowe's time. Despite all the strides that have been taken to "solve" these issues, they continue to be debated and discussed widely, from history books and classes to Twitter feeds.

Black Rights and Representation

Despite Stowe's best intentions, the name "Uncle Tom" in modern speech is best identified as an insult. It remains a standard epithet for a black person who behaves in a subservient manner toward white people and aids in the repression of his or her own race. It is also often associated with not owning a gun, and thus with the inability to defend oneself. In recent history, the term has been applied to Dr. Martin Luther King Jr., Supreme Court Justice

Clarence Thomas, former US Secretary of State Colin Powell, and even President Barack Obama.

Another issue at the heart of the novel is black representation and white privilege. Stowe's novel raises valid questions around the ability of a member of a particular race to represent another race. Can a true portrayal be created in such a case? Should it even be attempted? How does our race affect our stories? Is Stowe's voice still valid when she was neither enslaved nor black? Such questions have no easy answers, but they are still worth discussing.

Feminism and Women's Literary Contributions

Some critics of the early twentieth century were quick to dismiss female authors' works, including *Uncle Tom's Cabin*, as intellectually inferior, especially denigrating works that were sentimental or that focused on women's issues.

In past years, there has been a strong tradition within classic literature of devaluing women's literary contributions. Regulated to the ranks of "domestic" fiction, it was a common belief that women's literature could only deal with love, marriage, children and what was "inside the home." One particularly popular genre in Stowe's time was sentimental fiction, and it was here such themes were often found. Sentimental fiction was largely dismissed by male-dominated literature circles due to its tendency toward the melodramatic and emotional; however, the genre produced some of the biggest bestsellers of its day. Many of today's literary and narrative clichés are rooted in this genre, from candlelit bedside death scenes to daring elopements and devilish kidnappings. A key aspect of Stowe's success was her use of

Commonly named among the "Great American Novels," *The Adventures* of *Huckleberry Finn* features the use of frequent racial slurs and has been criticized for conforming to rather than challenging nineteenth-century racial stereotypes.

this genre to frame the narrative of *Uncle Tom's Cabin*. It presented what was a radical political act for its time in a "language" that could be most readily understood and appreciated by her audience.

Another criticism of Stowe has been her treatment of race. Yet, as author and critic Jane Smiley has noted, why is Stowe's novel treated more harshly than works written by men which are just as dated and offensive in their portrayals of African Americans? Why is *The Adventures of Huckleberry Finn* an American classic and *Uncle Tom's Cabin* an embarrassment to modern America? In her 1996 article for *Harper's* magazine, "Say It Ain't So, Huck: Second Thoughts on Mark Twain's 'Masterpiece,'" she argues:

> Ernest Hemingway, thinking of himself, as always, once said that all American literature grew out of *Huck Finn*. It undoubtedly would have been better for American literature, and American culture, if our literature had grown out of [*Uncle Tom's Cabin*] which for its portrayal of an array of thoughtful, autonomous, and passionate black characters leaves *Huck Finn* far behind … [Stowe] truly believed that all Americans together had to find a solution to the problem of slavery in which all were implicated. When her voice, a courageously public voice … fell silent in our culture and was replaced by the secretive voice of *Huck Finn*, who acknowledges Jim only when they are alone on the raft together out in the middle of the big river, racism fell out of the public world and into the private one, where whites think it really is but blacks know it really isn't.

1900–1950: The Backlash Begins

It was the criticism of the twentieth century that most clearly shaped our modern understanding of Stowe's work and her characters. While the majority of nineteenth-century critics effusively praised Stowe's pious characters and humanitarian fervor, the following decade took a more circumspect and critical stance. *Uncle Tom's Cabin* had sought to tackle the popular proslavery view of its time—that black people were inferior to white people—and took the decade's Christian morality as a symbol of the highest form of humanity there was. As a result of this, Tom's Christlike attitude and behavior elevated him and made him the moral superior of almost every white character in the narrative. For nineteenth-century America, this was revolutionary; however, by the start of the 1900s, black activists began more and more to reject such notions, wanting for the most part not to be equal by virtue of being superhuman, but by virtue of their own innate personhood whatever their behavior or beliefs.

One of the first modern writers to tackle this subject was the scholar W. E. B. Du Bois. Born in Massachusetts, Du Bois would eventually become the first African American to earn a doctorate from Harvard University. Du Bois was a prominent sociologist, historian, civil rights activist, and writer. In 1903, he published *The Souls of Black Folk*, a collection of essays on race that is now seen as one of the first works of sociology. The essential message of the book was that black people in the South needed the right to vote and the right to a good education, and deserved to be treated with equality and justice. Du Bois used the character of Tom as an example of how plantation life stunted ethical growth. He claimed that Tom's "deep religious fatalism" was symptomatic of a plantation slave's existence where "habits of shiftlessness took root, and sullen hopelessness replaced hopeful strife." In essence, Du Bois was addressing the great flaw that modern readers have perceived in Tom. In the words of the critic Hollis Robbins, they wanted Tom to "stop praying and serving and do something."

The Boston journalist Pauline Hopkins revisited *Uncle Tom's Cabin* from another angle in 1916. A pioneer of her time, Hopkins was a novelist, journalist, playwright, historian, and editor. She was deeply influenced by the work of Du Bois but blazed her own path using the romantic novel to explore social and racial themes. She was the inaugural editor of the nation's first African-American literary journal, the *Colored American Magazine*. She was particularly interested in the character of Topsy, the young slave girl placed in Miss Ophelia's care. Seeking to redress the wrongs done to the character, she published a serialized story about Topsy Templeton, an unrestrained young orphan of color who becomes the object of "rehabilitation" by two white, spinster sisters.

In 1949, James Baldwin published the most well-known and highly-regarded piece of *Uncle Tom* criticism in history with his essay "Everybody's Protest Novel." Baldwin was a novelist, essayist, playwright, poet, and social critic. He is best known for his novels, such as *Go Tell It on the Mountain* and *Giovanni's Room*. His

James Baldwin heavily criticized both *Uncle Tom's Cabin*'s depiction of African Americans and what he saw as the lengths that black literary characters had to go to in order to be "deserving" of respect and equality.

childhood experiences had left him with a deep mistrust of religion, and throughout his work, Baldwin often accused Christianity of reinforcing slavery by its attempts to soothe the pain of oppression without removing the cause, and for its belief in delaying salvation until a promised afterlife. This may explain to a degree Baldwin's impassioned reaction against the novel. He described it as containing "medieval morality" that revolved around contradictory constructions of "black, white, the devil, [and] the next world." Slamming the use of sentimentality, he instead argued that such conventions were "the mark of dishonesty, the inability to feel … and the signal of secret and violent inhumanity." Baldwin objected strongly to the notion that blacks should be passive in the face of white violence, noting that the "avowed aim of the American protest novel is to bring greater freedom to the oppressed." He firmly believed that Stowe's novel had not given Tom and his contemporaries that freedom, but rather constrained them further into "correct" behavior that must be followed in order to gain certain rights. Baldwin was further angered by the use of social and racial deaths that seemed prerequisites for protests to be palatable to white communities. To this day, Baldwin's analysis is still perceived to be one of the most eloquent and decisive critiques of Stowe's work and the agendas behind racial literature.

1951–2000: The Rise of the "Uncle Tom"

On the heels of Baldwin's criticism, it became more and more unfashionable to praise Stowe's work or her agenda, and the term "Uncle Tom" was increasingly used as an insult. In the 1960s, as power battles between different ideologies raged within the civil rights movement, the novel fell under the eyes of activist Malcolm X. A leading light of the religious group the Nation of Islam, Malcolm X was a controversial advocate for black rights. To some, he was a courageous and fearless critic, holding white America to account for its racial crimes in the strongest terms; yet others believed his speeches promoted racism and violence. Malcolm X used the novel to attack fellow civil rights campaigner Martin Luther King Jr., describing him as a "modern" Uncle Tom who was "doing the same thing today, to keep Negroes defenseless in the face of an attack."

Scholar Henry Louis Gates Jr. describes Uncle Tom's fall as follows:

> [W]ith the rise of popular black militancy in the 60's that poor old Uncle Tom became the quintessential symbol that separated the good black guys from the servile sellouts. He was the embodiment of "race betrayal," an object of scorn, a scapegoat for all of our political self-doubts.

In the 1970s, with the rise of feminism, scholars began to reclaim writers like Stowe and reevaluate their works. Critic Jane Tompkins praised Harriet Beecher Stowe as a feminist figure worthy of scholarly interest, examining the book not in terms of modern depictions of race but by examining what had come before and how Stowe used the contemporary context to create a work that would have the most significant political impact. The writer Joan Hedrick, who would win a Pulitzer Prize for her 1994 biography of Stowe, would further expand Tompkins's work.

Toward the end of the 1980s, slave narratives were reexamined and rewritten. In 1987, writer Toni Morrison released *Beloved*. Inspired by true events, the story follows Sethe, a runaway slave mother living in Ohio. Sethe's life begins on a plantation in Kentucky, but she soon

Writer Toni Morrison used her novel *Beloved* to explore the issue of slavery from the perspective of a slave mother driven to desperate lengths.

TWENTIETH-CENTURY ADAPTATIONS

During the 1900s, *Uncle Tom's Cabin* continued to be a controversial production for the film industry.

The first adaptation of the novel was a 1903 silent film by Edwin S. Porter. It was one of the first full-length movies, but it borrowed heavily from the tradition of "Tom shows." Porter cast white actors in blackface for leading black roles and only included black actors as extras. The film used numerous racist stereotypes, including one scene where the slaves dance at a slave auction.

There were numerous silent film adaptations made over the next two decades, but none managed to move the material forward until the 1927 version, directed by Harry A. Pollard. It was the third-most-expensive movie of the silent era, costing $1.8 billion. Black actor Charles Gilpin was initially cast in the title role but was later fired after the studio decided his portrayal was too aggressive. The role was then given to James B. Lowe. Black media outlets praised the film upon release, but later the studio became fearful of reprisals from white and Southern audiences. As a result, they cut controversial scenes, such as the opening scene of a slave auction where a slave mother is torn from her baby.

The most recent version was a television broadcast in 1987, which sought to redress the novel's original intentions. It starred Avery Brooks, Phylicia Rashad, and Samuel L. Jackson.

escapes with her children. After twenty-eight days on the run, slave catchers arrive to take Sethe and her children back. Sethe kills her two-year-old rather than allow her to be forced back into slavery. The aftermath of this horrific scene is where the story begins. It won the Pulitzer Prize for Fiction in 1988 and is often claimed as a modern classic. In contrast to Stowe's angelic slave mothers, Morrison and her contemporaries pulled no punches in portrayals of those women "who bear wicked burdens of flawed antebellum domesticity, unchecked white male desire, and an inhumane and dehumanizing marketplace."

2001 Onward

With the beginning of a new century, criticism around Stowe and her work has become more nuanced and complex. With the release of an annotated critical edition of *Uncle Tom's Cabin*, scholar and historian Henry Louis Gates Jr. refuted Baldwin's description of the novel as merely a "promotion of feminine tears and anguish as a form of political protest." Critic Veronica Margraves later highlighted modern audiences' lack of religious knowledge as a barrier to true understanding and appreciation for the style of characters of the novel, stating:

> Most Americans do not have the familiarity to the Bible nor use Christian imagery in everyday conversation as they did in Stowe's day, and this leads the modern reader to read scenes that seem overdramatic as idealistic, and thus they miss even the smallest religious imagery in the novel.

In 2012, David S. Reynolds published *Mightier Than the Sword*, a historical work tracing the factors that made *Uncle Tom's Cabin* "one of the most influential novels ever written by an American." His work also followed the aftermath of its publication and its adaptation through the years. When looking at popular criticisms of the novel, he singled out Baldwin's essay as a "blinkered critique," pointing to the fact that what seems now like "racial stereotyping" was "progressive" within Stowe's own time.

However history chooses to view Harriet Beecher Stowe, and however our perceptions of her and her most famous work may change over the decades, it is clear that the publication of *Uncle Tom's Cabin* was a historic moment in American history. It forever changed the course of race relations within the country as well as within literature, both American and further afield. Stowe once said: "Most mothers are instinctive philosophers." This may be true. The influence of Stowe's experience of motherhood as well as the shadow of her own mother, Roxana, shaped not only her responses to issues such as abolition, but also gave her an ability to connect with enslaved people on the basis of something as universal as family. While Uncle Tom may no longer have the reputation that Stowe intended for him, he continues to be a relevant and necessary character within the American canon and a figure that deserves closer inspection and greater understanding.

CHRONOLOGY

1811 Harriet Elizabeth Beecher is born in Litchfield, Connecticut, on June 14.

1824 Harriet moves to Hartford, Connecticut, to attend her sister's school, Hartford Female Seminary.

1832 At the age of twenty-one, Harriet moves to Cincinnati, Ohio, to join her father.

1833 Cincinnati is hit with a serious influenza epidemic.

1834 Harriet wins a writing contest in the *Western Monthly Magazine*.

1836 Riots break out in Cincinnati between African Americans and ethnic Irish migrants. Harriet marries Calvin Ellis Stowe and becomes Harriet Beecher Stowe.

1850 Southern states threaten to secede from the Union.

1851 First installment of *Uncle Tom's Cabin* is published in the *National Era* newspaper.

1852 *Uncle Tom's Cabin* is re-released as a novel.

1861 The first seven states secede from the Union and become the Confederate States of America. Confederates attack Fort Sumter, South Carolina, signaling the start of the American Civil War. Virginia, North Carolina, Arkansas, and Tennessee secede and join the Confederacy.

1862 General Robert E. Lee assumes command of the Confederate Army. Harriet Beecher Stowe meets Abraham Lincoln.

1863 The second half of the Emancipation Proclamation is issued, freeing all southern slaves. In November, Abraham Lincoln is reelected as president.

1865 The Fifteenth Amendment to abolish slavery is approved by Congress. General Lee surrenders to General Ulysses S. Grant after fleeing Petersburg. President Lincoln is shot in the head by John Wilkes Booth—he dies the next day. Confederate soldiers who have not yet surrendered now do so.

1870 Harriet Beecher Stowe opens an integrated school in Mandarin, Florida.

1896 Harriet Beecher Stowe dies in Hartford, Connecticut, at the age of eighty-five.

GLOSSARY

Alzheimer's disease A common disease among older people that results in the gradual loss of memory, speech, movement, and the ability to think clearly.

antebellum Referring to anything that occurred before the American Civil War.

codified To arrange something, such as laws or rules, into a system.

dehumanization To remove from a person the special human qualities of independent thought, feeling for other people, etc.

dementia A medical condition that affects especially the elderly, causing the memory and other mental abilities to gradually become worse, and leading to confused behavior.

deterrent Something that discourages people from doing something.

egalitarian Believing that all people are equally important and should have the same rights and opportunities in life.

emancipation The process of giving people social or political freedom and rights.

fatalism The belief that people cannot change the way events will happen and that events, especially bad ones, cannot be avoided.

frivolity Behavior that is silly and not serious, or things that are silly and not important.

grassroots activism Political activities carried out by the ordinary people in a society or an organization, especially a political party.

humanitarian A person who is involved in or connected with improving people's lives and reducing suffering.

innate A quality or ability that you were born with, not one you have learned.

literate Able to read and write.

melodramatic Showing much stronger emotions than are necessary or usual for a situation.

nationalism A nation's wish and attempt to be politically independent.

outfitting To provide someone or something with equipment or clothes.

paternalism Behavior that limits a person or group's liberty or autonomy for what is presumed to be that person or group's own good.

perplexity A state of confusion or a complicated and difficult situation or thing.

puritan Someone who believes that it is important to work hard and control oneself, and that pleasure is wrong or unnecessary.

reprisal Activity against another person, especially as a punishment by military forces or a political group.

republicanism The belief in government by elected representatives of the people rather than government by a king or queen.

revival A time when interest in religion starts again in a stronger way than before, or a meeting or series of meetings organized to encourage this to happen.

rhetoric Speech or writing intended to be effective and to influence people.

seminary A college for training people to become priests or ministers.

spiritualism The belief that living people can communicate with people who have died.

temperance The habit of not drinking alcohol because of the belief that it is dangerous or wrong.

theologian A person who studies religion and religious belief.

Underground Railroad A network of secret routes and safe houses designed to aid fugitive slaves to escape to free states or Canada. The system was supported and run by a combination of abolitionists and sympathetic supporters. The system was first created at the beginning of the nineteenth century and reached its peak between 1850 and 1860.

urbanize To build houses, offices, or other buildings in a rural area in order to develop the area.

SOURCES

CHAPTER ONE

pg. 10: Ferrell, Claudine. *The Abolitionist Movement*. (Westport, CT: Greenwood Publishing Group, 2006), p. 4.

pg. 12: Media Projects, Inc. *Student Almanac of African American History, Volume 1*. (Westport: Greenwood Publishing Group, 2003), p. 29.

pg. 18: Harrold, Stanley. *American Abolitionists*. (New York: Routledge, 2014), p. 3.

pg. 25: *Ibid.*

CHAPTER TWO

pg. 29-30: Hedrick, Joan D. *Harriet Beecher Stowe: A Life*. (New York: Oxford University Press, 1995), p. 32.

pg. 30: Beecher, Lyman. *Autobiography, Correspondence, Etc., of Lyman Beecher, Volume 2*. (New York: Harper & Brothers, 1886) p. 2.

pg. 35: Grant Wilson, James and John Fiske, *Appleton's Cyclopaedia of American* Biography. (New York: D. Appleton, 1888), p. 128.

pg. 36: Koester, Nancy. *Harriet Beecher Stowe: A Spiritual Life*. (Grand Rapids: William E. Eerdmans Publishing Company, 2014), p. 24.

pg. 38: Hedrick, p. 109.

pg. 38: Ascione, Frank R. *Child Abuse, Domestic Violence, and Animal Abuse*. (West Lafayette: Purdue University Press, 1999), p. 309.

pg. 39: Hedrick, p. 18.

pg. 41: Nicolay, John G. and John Hay. *Abraham Lincoln: Biographies*. (Golgotha Press, 2010), p. 23.

pg. 42: Homestead, Melissa J. *American Women Authors and Literary Property, 1822-1869*. (Cambridge: Cambridge University Press, 2005), p. 29.

pg. 43: Zinn, Howard. *A People's History of the United States: 1492–Present*. (Oxon: Routledge, 2013) p. 121.

pg. 45: "Rewriting Uncle Tom." *Washington Post* (Washington, DC, 1888) http://utc.iath.virginia.edu/articles/n2ar19cmt.html.

pg. 45: Krauth, Leland. *Mark Twain & Company: Six Literary Relations*. (Athens, GA: University of Georgia Press, 2003), p. 92.

CHAPTER THREE

pg. 51: Bremner, Robert Hamlett. *Children and Youth in America: 1600-1865.* (Cambridge: Harvard University Press, 1970), p. 377.

pg. 54: Cantarow, Ellen. *Moving the Mountain: Women Working for Social Change*. (New York: Feminist Press, 1980) p. xxxv.

pg. 57: Hedrick, p. 56.

pg. 57: Hedrick, p. 11.

pg. 58: *The Slave's Friend, vol.1, no.7*. (New York: American Anti-Slavery Society, 1836), p. 4-5.

pg. 58: Carter, Greg. *The United States of the United Races: A Utopian History of Racial Mixing*. (New York: New York University Press, 2013), p. 59.

pg. 61: Kelley, Mary. '"Feeling Right": Harriet Beecher Stowe, *Uncle Tom's Cabin*, and the Power of Sympathy' (http://utc.iath.virginia.edu/interpret/exhibits/kelley/kelley.html).

pg. 61: Bodenhamer, David J. *Our Rights*. (Oxford: Oxford University Press, 2007), p. 44.

CHAPTER FOUR

pg. 64: Lindley, Susan Hill. *You Have Stepped Out of Your Place: A History of Women and Religion*. (Louisville, KY: Westminster John Knox Press, 1996), p. 111.

pg. 64: Boynton, Claudia Wolfe. *Remarkable Women of Hartford*. (Charleston, SC: The History Press, 2014), p. 36.

pg. 66-67: Phelgey, Jennifer & Janet Badia. *Reading Women: Literary Figures and Cultural Icons from the Victorian Age to the Present*. (Toronto: University of Toronto Press, 2005), p. 67.

pg. 70: Beecher Stowe, Harriet. *Uncle Tom's Cabin*. (London: George Routledge & Co., 1852), p. 33.

pg. 71: *Ibid.*, p. 7.

CHAPTER FIVE

pg. 79: Lester, Charles Edwards. *Life and Public Services of Charles Sumner*. (New York: United States Publishing Co., 1874) p. 155.

pg. 81: Meer, Sarah. *Uncle Tom Mania: Slavery, Minstrelsy, and Transatlantic Culture in the 1850s*. (Athens, GA: The University of Georgia Press, 2005), p. 179.

pg. 81: *Edinburgh Review, or Critical Journal, Volumes 101-102*. (New York: Leonard Scott & Co., 1855), p. 165.

pg. 83: Levine, Robert S. *Martin Delany, Frederick Douglass, and the Politics of Representative Identity*. (Chapel Hill, NC: The University of North Carolina Press, 2000), p. 21.

pg. 84: Beecher Stowe, p. 566.

pg. 84: Watkins, Frances E. "To Mrs. Harriet Beecher Stowe." *Frederick Douglass Paper* (Rochester, NY: 27 January 1854).

pg. 85: Sundquist, Eric J. *New Essays on Uncle Tom's Cabin*. (Cambridge: Cambridge University Press, 1993), p. 68.

pg. 87: Cooper, Afua. *My name is Henry Bibb: A Story of Slavery and Freedom*. (New York: KCP Fiction, 2009), p. 50.

pg. 87: *Ibid.*, p. 56.

pg. 88-89: Cooper, Louisa Susanna. *Political and Social Essays*. (Charlottesville, VA: University Press of Virginia, 1995), p. 277.

pg. 92: Du Bois, W. E. B. & David Levering Lewis. *Black Reconstruction in America 1860-1880*. (New York: The Free Press, 1992), p. 109.

pg. 92: Brown, Lois. *African American Responses to* Uncle Tom's Cabin. (http://utc.iath.virginia.edu/interpret/exhibits/brown/brown.html).

pg. 92: *Ibid.*

pg. 93: *Ibid.*

pg. 93: Cooper, Afua, p. 61.

pg. 93: Brown, William Wells. *The Anthology of Early African American Literature*. (Golgatha, 2013), p. 45.

CHAPTER SIX

pg. 97: Hughes, Langston. *The Collected Works of Langston Hughes: Essays on Art, Race, Politics, and World Affairs, Vol. 9*. (Columbia, MO: University of Missouri Press), p. 490.

pg. 97: Cushman, Thomas. *George Orwell: Into the Twenty-first Century*. (Oxon, UK: Routledge, 2016), p. 221.

pg. 98: Robbins, Hollis. 'Uncle Tom's Cabin and the Matter of Influence.' *The Gilder Lehman Institute of American History*. (https://www.gilderlehrman.org/history-by-era/literature-and-language-arts/essays/uncle-tom%E2%80%99s-cabin-and-matter-influence).

pg. 101: Warren, Joyce W. *Challenging Boundaries: Gender and Periodization*. (Athens, GA: The University of Georgia Press, 2000), p. 30.

pg. 102: Johnson, Brian. *Du Bois on Reform: Perodical-based Leadership for African Americans*. (Oxford: Alta Mira Press, 2005), p. xxii.

pg. 102: Robbins, Hollis. *In Search of Hannah Crafts: Critical Essays on the Bondwoman's Narrative*. (BasicCivitas, 2004), p. 319.

pg. 104: Gayle, Addison. *The Addison Gayle Jr.* Reader. (Chicago: The University of Illinois Press, 2009), p. 112.

pg. 104: Starkey, Brando Simeo. *In Defense of Uncle Tom*. (New York: Cambridge University Press, 2015), p. 197.

pg. 104: Gates, Henry Louis Jr. 'Cabin Fever.' *The New York Times*. (http://www.nytimes.com/2006/10/22/books/review/Gates.t.html?pagewanted=print&_r=0).

pg. 107: Brown, Lois. *African American Responses to* Uncle Tom's Cabin. (http://utc.iath.virginia.edu/interpret/exhibits/brown/brown.html).

pg. 107: Gates, Henry Louis Jr. "Cabin Fever." *The New York Times*. (http://www.nytimes.com/2006/10/22/books/review/Gates.t.html?pagewanted=print&_r=0).

pg. 107: Margraves, Veronica. "Rethinking Contemporary Criticism of *Uncle Tom's Cabin*: Unraveling the Myth of Transparency." (https://www2.cortland.edu/dotAsset/123942.pdf).

pg. 108: Reynolds, David S. *Mightier Than The Sword: Uncle Tom's Cabin and the Battle for America*. (New York: W. W. Norton, 2012), p. 5.

pg. 108: Beecher Stowe, Harriet. *Stowe: Three Novels*. (New York: The Library of America, 1982), p. 721.

FURTHER INFORMATION

BOOKS

Haugen, Brenda. *Harriet Beecher Stowe: Author and Advocate*. Mankato, MN: Capstone Publishers, 2005.

Hochman, Barbara. *Uncle Tom's Cabin and the Reading Revolution: Race, Literacy, Childhood, and Fiction, 1851-1911*. Amherst, MA: University of Massachusetts Press, 2011.

Koester, Nancy. *Harriet Beecher Stowe: A Spiritual Life*. Grand Rapids, MI: Wm. B. Eerdmans Publishing, 2014.

Jordan-Lake, Joy. *Whitewashing Uncle Tom's Cabin: Nineteenth-Century Women Novelists Respond to Stowe*. Nashville, TN: Vanderbilt University Press, 2005.

Mayer, Sylvia. *Beyond Uncle Tom's Cabin: Essays on the Writing of Harriet Beecher Stowe*. Madison, NJ: Fairleigh Dickinson University Press, 2011.

WEBSITES

BBC Radio 4 — In Our Time: Uncle Tom's Cabin
www.bbc.co.uk/radio/player/p003c1bp

Radio program discussing *Uncle Tom's Cabin* and its impact on the Civil War, the abolition of slavery, and stereotypes of African-Americans.

The Gilder Lehrman Institute of American History
www.gilderlehrman.org

Online historical database including critical articles, seminars, and primary sources.

Harriet Beecher Stowe Center
www.harrietbeecherstowecenter.org

Resource site for the Harriet Beecher Stowe Center Museum, containing information on Stowe's life, family, and the book *Uncle Tom's Cabin*.

Uncle Tom's Cabin & American Culture: A Multi-Media Archive
utc.iath.virginia.edu

Electronic archive with access to primary sources, historical background materials, online editions of the novel, and critical essays.

Worcester Women's History Project
www.wwhp.org/Resources/Slavery

Official website of volunteer organization dedicated to raising awareness of the first National Women's Rights Convention and the lives of its supporters.

MUSEUMS

Harriet Beecher Stowe House
77 Forest St, Hartford, CT 06105, United States

www.harrietbeecherstowecenter.org/visit/hbs_house.shtml

Harriet Beecher Stowe House
2950 Gilbert Ave, Cincinnati, OH 45206, United States

www.stowehousecincy.org/

Uncle Tom's Cabin Historic Site
Ontario Heritage Trust
29251 Uncle Toms Rd, Dresden, ON N0P 1M0, Canada

www.heritagetrust.on.ca/Uncle-Tom-s-Cabin-Historic-Site/Home.aspx

BIBLIOGRAPHY

Adams, Ephraim Douglass. *Great Britain and the American Civil War*. New York, NY: Diversion Books, 2014.

Brown, Lois. "African American Responses to *Uncle Tom's Cabin*." Accessed January 20, 20016 (utc.iath.virginia.edu/interpret/exhibits/brown/brown.html).

Buell, Tonya. *Slavery in America: A Primary Source History of the Intolerable Practice of Slavery*. New York: The Rosen Publishing Group, 2003.

Du Bois, W. E. B. *The Souls of Black Folk*. Auckland, NZ: The Floating Press, 2010.

Ferrell, Claudine. *The Abolitionist Movement*. Westport, CT: Greenwood Publishing Group, 2006.

Harrold, Stanley. *American Abolitionists*. London: Routledge, 2014.

Hedrick, Joan D. *Harriet Beecher Stowe: A Life*. Oxford, UK: Oxford Paperbacks, 1995.

Henson, Josiah. *The Life of Josiah Henson, Formerly A Slave, Now an Inhabitant of Canada, as Narrated by Himself*. Charleston, SC: BiblioBazaar, 2009.

Newman, Richard S. *The Transformation of American Abolitionism: Fighting Slavery in the Early Republic*. Chapel Hill, NC: University of North Carolina Press, 2002.

Phegley, Jennifer and Janet Badia. *Reading Women: Literary Figures and Cultural Icons from the Victorian Age to the Present*. Toronto, ON: University of Toronto Press, 2005.

Reynolds, David S. *Mightier Than The Sword: Uncle Tom's Cabin and the Battle for America*. New York: W. W. Norton & Company, 2011.

Sonneborn, Liz. *Harriet Beecher Stowe*. New York: Infobase Learning, 2013.

Walvin, James. *A Short History of Slavery*. London: Penguin UK, 2007.

Weinstein, Cindy. *The Cambridge Companion to Harriet Beecher Stowe*. Cambridge, UK: Cambridge University Press, 2004.

INDEX

Page numbers in **boldface** are illustrations. Entries in **boldface** are glossary terms.

ABOUT THE AUTHOR

Katie Griffiths is a long-time history buff and has written several nonfiction books for middle- and high-school students on history, culture, and mythology. For more information, visit www.katiegriffiths.net.